Mastering

Your
Trading

Learn from Expert Trading Advisors

By: Larry Jacobs

ISBN-13: 978-1515176886

ISBN-10: 1515176886

TABLE OF CONTENTS

r

INTRODUCTION

Traders World created a magazine for traders' some 28 years ago. The magazine now goes out to thousands of subscribers in all 30 countries. We have also produced over 17 Traders World Online Expos featuring presentations from the top traders of the world for the last 5 years.

This book contains articles from the presenters of our current Traders World Online Expo #17. For this expo the presenting traders created both a video presentation and a written version of it for this book to help your better understand and trade the markets for profits.

Successful trading is a learned discipline. To be successful a trader you need to find an edge that puts you above the rest of the pack.

In this book you are presented many strategies and methods from many successful traders and from these you might be able to put together ideas to:

Mastering Your Trading

Here, with all the dogmatism of brevity, are some of the ways that you might get a trading edge from these articles and audio-visual presentations.

1. First read the entire book and find which strategies or methods of trading that best fit your own style. Everyone is different and what works for me probably won't work for you. Everyone has a

different personality. Don't try to trade like me or anyone else, trade like you.

2. Next go to the Traders World Online Expo site and then listen to the presentations. They are listed in the back of this book. Listen to the ones that best fit your own idea of how the markets work. If necessary listen to them several times and take notes. Taking notes will help you better understand what you are hearing and seeing.

Go here for the current expo.

http://www.tradersworldonlineexpo.com/

3. Next contact the companies or individuals that produced the articles and presentations that you liked the best. Ask as many questions as you can to understand what they have and what it can do for you. Ask for historical track records if they are available. See if they have testimonials.

4. See if a trial is available for 30-days for you to test what they have. Test it on historical data. Go back as far as possible so you can and see what the method can do. See when it succeeded and failed on past data and try to understand why.

5. Now test the strategy or method on real live data for as long as you can. Paper trade and pretend it is real money and record your results. Act that this is real money so the psychology is there. Many traders can successfully paper trade, but when they start to trade with real money, they fail. You don't what that to happen to you. Keep accurate records of your paper trading and remember to use money management. Don't trade with real-money until you

are completely profitable paper trading. It may take you several weeks, months or even years before you are profitable. Don't rush in to real trading till you are ready.

6. Finally when you are confident that you can trade profitably start small and work your way up with larger positions and as I said before use money management. Keep accurate records of your trading and what you saw and the reasons behind each trade. Make a screen shot of the chart when you initiated the position and when you liquidated it.

7. Keep searching to improve your edge, even if you have found something that gives you that trading edge you were looking for. Continue to do research that might even improve what you have. Never stop looking. Never be content with what you have.

8. To help you get started I have a free gift for you in mastering your trading. You can access the videos in expo #17. Go here to register and access the videos:

http://tradersworldonlineexpo.com/contact_form/

9. Remember that trading is risky. Please fully understand the methods and strategies you are using as well as the markets be before you trade. This book is for educational purposes only. Treat trading as a business. See our Disclaimer at the end of this book

Chapter 1 - Price and Volume the Only True Leading Indicators by Joel Pozen

Richard Ney said if you want to know the inventory objectives of professionals watch how they use price to influence volume. Contrary to popular misconception price leads volume. Contrary to popular misconception, high volume tends to be a reversal signal of price not continuation of price.

"The 'professional' should be thought of as a merchant with some rather unique inventory problems and opportunities. His goal, always, is to buy at wholesale prices and to sell at retail. This applies to his actions in the course of trading day as well as a year of trading." Richard Ney

Are YOU WILLING to do something different to HAVE something different?

Learn a strategy that will enable you to buy wholesale on DOWN BARS and sell retail on UP BARS, just like the pros do. Doing so enables you to use the TIGHTEST STOPS in trading, providing you with a remarkable risk reward ratio.

Learn a formula to determine margin that makes 50% per month in the market of your choice.

It's practical, hands-on training that you can apply immediately.

The SIMPLICITY of PRICE and VOLUME

2 Sell Signals on EUR/USD

5/1/15

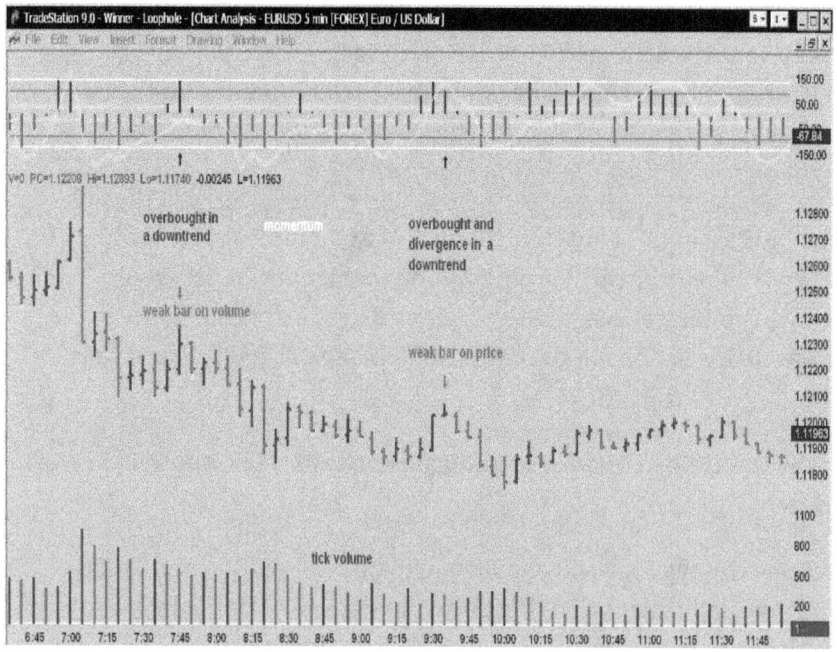

You Have Not Been Told the Truth About the Markets!

Dear Fellow Trader,

The Truth is: Markets Are Manipulated...

Before his death in 2004, Richard Ney, was the foremost expert on market manipulation. None other than J. Paul Getty, the world's richest man when he died, trusted Richard Ney to trade his money. Because he publicly called the crash of 1962, Mr. Ney was on the cover of Time Magazine. He subsequently called every market crash until his death. He wrote 3 New York Times bestsellers (which you will hear about on the webinar) along with exposing a little known 1963 congressional report stating that insiders have control of the markets, particularly at the open and close.

25 years ago Richard Ney taught me that markets are nothing more than merchandising mechanisms run by thieves who do their absolute best to separate as much money, from as many people as possible, in the least amount of time. The markets were set up to transfer money from the many to the few: from amateurs to professionals. Markets don't move. They are moved by the inventory objectives of professionals so they can buy at wholesale and sell at retail.

"I align myself with the specialist as he seeks to solve his inventory problems. The thrust of all my efforts is to buy when he buys and to sell when he sells."

No one else is revealing to the public Mr. Ney's knowledge and wisdom regarding reading price and volume, the true leading indicators.

You'll discover a simple and proven low-risk method that you'll quickly grasp. You'll learn how those with money put money to work to make money. It doesn't matter if you are totally new to trading or have been trading for years, you'll learn what the pros know and how you can take that knowledge and apply it. And these principles work in any market - stocks, commodities, futures, etfs, currencies, etc......and in any time frame.

The presentation you are about to attend discloses information you won't find in any conventional financial publication. In fact, you'll be hard pressed to find this information anywhere because professionals/insiders don't want you doing what they do to take money out of the markets. Once you understand how professionals manipulate prices, you can:

a.. Recognize Their Patterns

b.. Duplicate Their Actions

c.. Achieve Extraordinary Results

WHEN ELEPHANTS WALK ACROSS YOUR LAWN THEY LEAVE
FOOTPRINTS

The elephants are the professionals/insiders and the lawn is a
price and volume chart.

**The Price-Volume Method is How the Market is Designed to
Work!**

Trading is not complicated. People make it that way! If you are
looking for complicated you will never see simple! It is ironic in
that trading is the biggest business in the world yet the least
understood. Those who control the market have a vested interest
in keeping it that way.

Every day, on price and volume charts, the market manipulation
of the select few leaves footprints. The way to succeed in the
market is to follow their footprints. Imagine how great it will be to
trade with confidence and obtain the amazing results that
previously were the domain of the moneyed elite. While you can't
change how the market works, you CAN "piggyback" the
'professionals' movements.

Professionals have no interest in your financial welfare. Price and
volume analysis tells you why the market is either trending up or
down. As your skills develop you will get a feel for what the
market is telling you. Price and volume analysis give you an edge
by training you to act correctly: to act in accordance with your
best financial interest.

Do not be influenced by advice from well meaning friends, brokers or the news. The only truth is price. Only believe your charts. Your charts tell you what has really happened. Charts never lie. Charts can not be manipulated. Simply ask the right questions by knowing what you are looking at and for. What better way to trade than to want what the market wants? Everything you need to know is on a simple price and volume chart.

When you know how to trade, trades will find you. Pattern recognition will dramatically improve your trading results and transform your life!

"Once you are able to recognize the existence of a chart formation, it should be possible for you to ascertain which professional merchandising procedure is underway and what consequences are likely to follow from it. The chart formations have as their common link the provision of "points of opportunity", that is, in an accumulation structure, several opportunities for professionals and other exchange insiders to add to their investment accounts, and in a distribution structure several opportunities to distribute and sell stock short." Richard Ney

Creating the wealth and prosperity you deserve is simply a matter of pattern recognition. A matter of making sound professional trading decisions based on foresight, not hindsight - a matter of anticipating market movement.

By attending the presentation you'll find out about a system that can make you the confident, disciplined trader that Wall (FRAUD) Street would rather you not become. It's practical, hands-on training that you can apply immediately.

Don't continue to be victimized by others looking to gain at your expense! At the presentation you will discover what few people know about protecting and growing money! Find out how professional traders build wealth for themselves!

Do You Want to Retire On Time and On Budget?
Do You Want to Protect and Grow Your Wealth?
Do You Want to Avoid Future Market Crashes?
Do You Want to Take Control of Your Financial Future?
...Of course you do. Everyone does.

You don't have to continue to rely on others because you don't think you can create your own wealth. There is a solution. You can achieve your income and retirement goals. The markets offer amazing wealth-building opportunities, but only if you understand how they work.

You can be part of the many or 1 of the few!

Richard Ney said:

"I buy when other people are selling."
That is exactly what professionals do and amateurs don't do.

After this presentation you'll be able to re-write your script with money. You'll be able to change your relationship with money. You'll learn things about the markets you never knew. Your opinion of the markets will never be the same.

http://www.besttradingstrategiesrevealed.com/
prosperitytrading@roadrunner.com

Chapter 2 - Uncovering Market Secrets with Machine Learning and Data Science by Dwayne Paschall

What Is Machine Learning?

Machine learning is the task of using statistical methods to find new insight into your data. It evolved from the fields of pattern recognition and artificial intelligence. Today, machine learning is often thought of as finding new algorithms to make predictions about your data. In our case, we're using advanced statistical analysis to discover hidden patterns, predict price movements, manage risk and increase profits for our trading. Since machine learning is a rule-based algorithm that "learns" new information from your data, machine learning and algorithmic trading fit well together and can be used hand in hand.

AutoTrade Signal has studied the markets for many years and has developed a suite of machine learning tools for traders. These tools add insight to your trading decisions. However, this approach is sometimes overlooked by traders.

Why?

Machine learning tools simplify trading decisions, price movement and technical analysis. In short, it makes trading more clear, rather than adding another suite of technical indicators on top of your already cluttered screen. In fact, we're developing a completely "indicator-less" trading platform for some of our advanced clients. That's right – no bivy of technical indicators smattered across the screen; no analysis of price movement (which is really just a very simplified version of more sophisticated statistical analysis), just the analysis of today's market and tomorrow's probabilities.

Wouldn't it be valuable to your trading to have deeper insight and clearer vision about tomorrow? This is precisely the value of machine learning tools for traders, even if you do not use any algorithmic strategies.

Noise Reduction

The first tool that we use is an analysis that removes the "noise" from price movement. In Figure 1 we see a typical candlestick chart of GS. Even if you only plot this screen on your chart, it contains ALOT of information: movement of daily opening prices, movement of daily closing prices, daily directional movement (green vs. red bar color), as well as the daily price range in the wicks of the candlesticks. In our analysis of how traders use this information, they basically all used the same visual cues: the candlestick showed them how the closing price moved up and down over time.

In order to aid in understanding price movements over time, we have developed a Noise Reduction Algorithm. When applied to the closing price of a stock, ETC or Futures contract, it is much easier to interpret what price is really doing.

The Noise Reduction algorithm has two essential features: 1) it reduces the market "noise" while preserving the major peaks and valleys and 2) it does this with ZERO LAG. Lets view an example of the Noise Reduction algorithm below. Figure 1 shows the typical candlestick plot of GS from July 2014 through late May 2015. As can be seen, the "true movement" of price is much easier to see, interpret and follow compared to the candlestick plot. That is because the candlestick chart is packed full of information that doesn't always make it easy to interpret. Also, the candlestick charting of raw market data includes a significant amount of "noise" – price movements that reverse or don't continue over the short term. This is one of the reasons why many people believe that market prices are random.

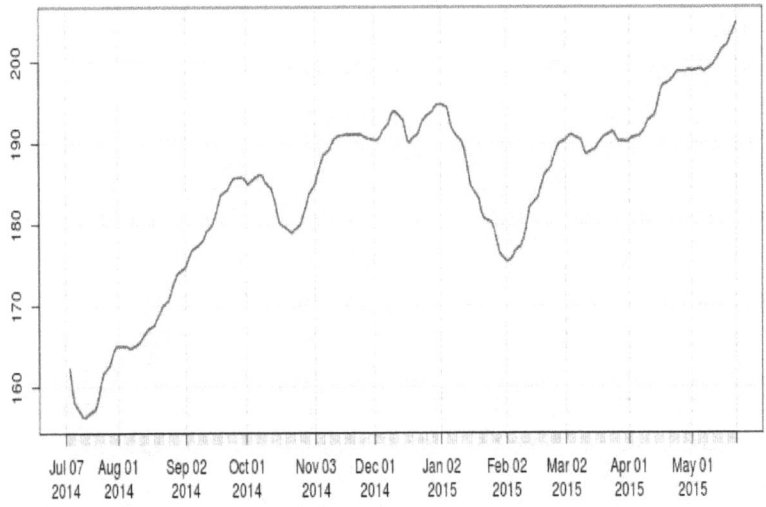

Noise Redux - Closing Price

Figure 1. Typical candlestick chart of GS

Figure 2. The same price series, same dates, but with the "noise" removed.

Predict Tomorrow's Price Change

One of the most important items traders wonder about is what price will do tomorrow. Will prices increase? Will prices decrease? There are numerous technical indicators that attempt to capture this information. In addition, many combinations of indicators also attempt to measure this price move for the next trading day.

We have developed a very power, yet easy to understand model of price prediction performance. By leveraging a series of sophisticated machine learning models, we can show you how likely it is for price to increase (+1) or decrease (-1) tomorrow. Figures 3 and 4 below show the output for one stock (AAPL) and one ETF (QQQ).

The information is very clear and easy to see. In Figure 3, the model indicates that AAPL has a probability or likelihood of 76 out of 100 that its closing price will increase tomorrow. Conversely, it predicts that only 24 out of 100 times it will decrease tomorrow.

In Figure 4, the model predicts that for QQQ, there is likelihood of 68 out of 100 that price will go Down tomorrow. Both of these cases show a pretty strong indication of where price is headed tomorrow. No guessing or interpreting 3-5 different technical indicators (which may not all agree with each other). Just a very clear presentation of how likely price is to increase or decrease tomorrow. If you knew the stock, ETF or futures contract has a likelihood of almost 80% that it will increase tomorrow, you would feel much more confident in your trading decisions.

```
                     -1      1

Probabilities:  0.24  0.76
```

Figure 3. Tomorrow's prediction for AAPL

	-1	1
Probabilities:	0.68	0.32

Figure 4. Tomorrow's prediction for QQQ

Conversely, if your trading strategy showed a weak signal to perhaps take a long position, but tomorrows prediction showed only a 48 out of 100 probability price would increase......I would definitely think twice about trading that weak signal. This is one of the strong points of using machine learning tools to assist your trading. It takes a lot of the guess work out of trading and gives clearer insight and understanding about what price is doing today, and is likely to do tomorrow.

Indicator Analysis

One of the more fascinating applications of machine learning that is often overlooked is the ability to discover which indicators are helpful to use in trading certain stocks, ETFs or futures contracts. I have talked with many traders who "...like to trade Oil..." or Facebook or day trade options on AAPL. That is all fine as long as the tools you use are the best ones for the task. Let me explain what I mean:

Below are the output of a machine learning model that measures the effectiveness of a whole list of technical indicators. It answers the following question: "which indicators are most powerful for telling me which direction, up or down, the price of this stock, ETF or futures contract will move?". Wouldn't you like to know that if you want to day trade FB or AAPL options that your trading strategy was using the most power technical indicators that correspond to price changes in the stock, ETF or futures contract?

In Figure 5 we show the relative indicator importance for two stocks, GS and MMM. For those of you who trade "price action" strategies, pay particular attention here. For GS (left column), Volume was among the most important indicators of price movement. However for MMM (right column), Volume was not among the most powerful indicators of price movement. So if you trade price action strategies, you may find yourself wondering why the system works better with GS than with MMM.

If you had used machine learning to guide your trading, you would have known that Volume would be more powerful for GS and less so for MMM BEFORE you ever traded a single dollar. However, if you look at MMM, you'll see that SMI is among the most powerful indicators for this stock. GS, however, was much less reactive using the SMI indicator.

So rather than using trail-and-error to select your portfolio, it would make more sense to know BEFORE you ever traded which indicators work best for the instruments you wish to trade. This is precisely what we have done for traders is to provide this information for every stock that's listed and traded in US markets. By using the most powerful indicators, you significantly reduce trades that don't work out.

	Overall		Overall
GS.Volume	102.69	MMM.Open	88.78
GS.Open	90.43	SMI	84.22
GS.Close.EMA.9	83.00	MMM.High	82.93
GS.High	80.13	MMM.Low	79.24
tr	78.29	MMM.Volume	78.93
GS.Close.2	78.19	MMM.Close.EMA.9	77.69
GS.Close.1	73.28	signal	76.83
mfi	71.46	MMM.Close.3	75.21
GS.Low	70.26	MMM.Close	74.99
cci	70.03	DX	72.32
SMI	69.69		
emv	67.72		

Figure 5. Relative importance of technical indicators for GS and MMM

Market News Sentiment

The last tool we will present is the news sentiment analysis tool. In this case, we scour the web for news stories about each of the major markets. We then compile all the current news and measure the sentiment, or "feeling" about that market. The current market sentiment is shown as a range of -5 to +5. Negative numbers represent negative feelings or sentiment and positive numbers represent positive feelings. The more positive the number, the more positive the sentiment. Simple.

Why is this important?

Even though your particular stock or ETF may have a positive prediction, its never a good idea to trade against the overall larger market. This is because regardless of how well or poor an individual company is doing, their price is often pushed around by the larger market.

To make this easier for traders, we calculate our own sentiment values and display them in an easy-to-read format (see Figure 6). This is really helpful if you're considering a trade but aren't sure. Take a quick look at the market sentiment for that segment and see what the general feeling is for that market. Then simply make sure you're not "swimming upstream" against the current.

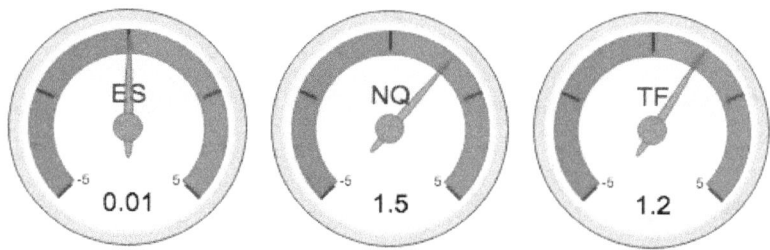

Figure 6. The current news sentiment or "feeling" about 3 markets

Machine Learning Work Flow

With all of the machine learning tools we presented, it would be helpful to also organize them into a single, logical work flow for

Price Chart   Tomorrow's Predictions   Most Important Indicators   Sentiment Gauges

traders. We have put together each of these tools and made them available in a single web-based format that makes using machine learning as easy and powerful as the underlying algorithms.

Figure 7. Machine Learning work flow tabs show us what information is most important for our trades.

Above is the Left-to-Right work flow that we use at AutoTrade Signal to trade with the powerful insight of machine learning. First, we check the Price Chart that shows closing price that has removed the market noise. Often, we will look at price over several date ranges. Next, we look to see what Tomorrow's Predictions will be. If price is predicted to increase, and the probability is greater than 0.65, we often consider taking this trade. The market Sentiment Gauges tell us if the trade is in concert with the over-riding market sentiment. If market sentiment doesn't go against our predicted trade direction, this is another indication of a price move in our direction. If we do have a particular trading strategy we've used in the past, we will often check the Most Important Indicators to see if our strategy uses the same indicators that are important for indicating price changes in the stock or ETF that we're considering. If so, we may take a look to see if the trading strategy also indicates a signal. IF not, however, we often leave the strategy closed down and don't even consult it. We have learned that unless the strategy is based on the SAME indicators that are most powerful in registering or showing price movements of the stock or ETF ahead of time, then it is often just confusing information that many times will keep us out of profitable trades, or put us in a trade that goes against our position.

Dwayne Paschall

dwaynepaschall@gmail.com

CHAPTER 3- MASTERING THE FEAR OF ALL FEARS IN TRADING – THE FEAR OF THE UNKNOWN BY J RANDE HOWELL

"I can see hijacking in hindsight, but not in the moment as I am trading. I'm in full control until after the fact when the thief has already come and gone and robbed me blind, again. Then I notice it, but I don't see the thief coming. If I had known he was coming, I would be prepared – but that's not the way it works. Before I know it, something takes over my mind and I am no longer in my right mind to trade. It's puzzling – it is so subtle that I can't detect it. I only see the aftermath of the poor decision-making in my trading account."

Why You Get Blind Sided Time and Time Again

Intellectually many people know how to trade. But, like the trader quoted above, this does not make them consistently profitable traders. Often their very "smartness" becomes a serious barrier to achieving success in trading. On the surface that's really counter-intuitive. After all, we are taught that being bright and knowledgeable and taking control of the situation is the ticket needed for success. Yet every day we see smart, knowledgeable traders fail in trading.

How can this be? The truth is that most traders are missing essential skills for success in trading – and they don't see that they are missing the skills. The very desirable trait of being smart blinds them from seeing other criteria just as necessary for consistent success. Yet, the trader's smartness precludes them from seeing what they need to see in the time frame they need to see it. In the explanation of the trader in the vignette above, that's the very clever thief who keeps stealing the trader blind. So smartness (both high IQ and knowledge) applied to trading can be both bad and good.

To be useful in trading, smartness has to be harnessed to help pull rather than lead. Or as Albert Einstein noted [paraphrased] the rational mind was the servant and the emotional mind the gift. He further observed that we get it wrong by ignoring the emotional mind and giving all the credit to the rational mind – the proverbial cart before the horse, much to our own detriment. Nowhere is this more obvious than in trading.

Understanding the Thief in the Trader's Mind – the Fear of the Unknown

First, let's start with the brain. The brain is an enormously adaptive organ constantly attuning the body to successfully negotiate survival with environmental experience. Electrical patterns, not thoughts, are the language of the brain as it negotiates this individual dance with life. Before symbols, sounds, smells, or feelings is this bio-electrical language that precedes the mind's language as thought. As the mind arises out of the brain's language, humans begin to think. But it is this primitive chemistry that is the primal force behind taking action under pressure.

So underneath all of this elegance of the rational mind is a brain running on electrical patterns with a mandate for self-preservation in the short term. This is the basis of the emotional brain from which thought arises. Depending on how the emotional brain sees a given situation, it is going to dictate how the rational mind is going to explain it. The thinking brain is not independent of the emotional brain. Rather it serves the emotional brain by producing explanations that support whatever decision it has already made. The thoughts and possibilities you perceive at any given moment are governed by the emotional state that currently controls the brain in that moment. Emotional decisions made under pressure make sense in the moment based on ancient survival mandates, but not after short term survival instincts cease triggering the fight/flight response.

This is why the trader in the vignette didn't see the thief coming. It was an inside job. The emotional brain of the trader had already made a decision and all the thinking mind could do was to produce an alibi that supported that decision. And the story of being "smart" clouded the trader's ability to get at the problem in his performance. "Smart" was the alibi that covered up the evidence that the thief was at the crime scene. The trader believed he was smart (and by IQ standards, he was) and that bias blinded him from seeing what was going on right in right of his eyes. He was simply too smart for his own good.

Learning How to See What You Are Blind to – Turning Toward the Unknown

Until the trader could look at himself with new eyes he was stuck in this vicious cycle. Prior to trading, his pattern (remember that the pattern was electrical long before it was thought and belief) was to get every last drop out of a deal. At one time this was not an established pattern. It was simply a solution that he fell into during a critical moment in his professional life prior to trading – and it worked. This solution had worked for him under pressurized situations for many years and had evolved into a deeply habituated pattern of survival and financial success. And it made him a successful business man.

And like successful emotional patterns will do, it naturally migrated to his trading style when he expanded his business into trading. The problem is that it didn't work in trading no matter how successful it was in business success. The markets were different than the other side of a negotiation – they didn't care one way or the other. No matter how much pressure he exerted on the other side of the trade, there was not give and take, like in business. Now the trader was simply fighting himself – hence the thief in the night.

What had been a very useful adaptation to a tough situation at one moment in time and a successful solution to building a successful business from the ground up over time had turned against him in trading. Suddenly the urgency to get every last little drop out of a deal was hijacking his capacity to produce success on the level he sought in trading.

Notice that at one time his brain simply tried out this success strategy as a possible solution, and it had worked. In truth it was a pressurized situation where he negotiated a hard deal and was fortunate enough to win. That didn't lock in the pattern, but it did set the process in motion. After many reps of this solution it was hardwired into pattern and came to be considered a personality trait. He became a tough negotiator under the stress of business negotiations.

Because it was historically so successful for such a long time, it became a familiar pattern that easily fired when engaging uncertainty and the similarity of the stress existing in business negotiations and the trading environment (where nothing is certain). The commonness of the pattern caused it to be pushed under the radar of the trader's awareness. It became a hidden assumption or belief that drove thinking during stressful moments. Until it was brought into awareness, it simply operated on instinct as pattern. If it were not for his trading account showing that there was a problem somewhere based on his trading results, it would have continued to go unnoticed.

Then his need to control uncertainty was uncovered – the fear of the unknown. The unknown is a threat to the current organization of the Self. Disorganization would mean death to the emotional brain and amygdala. So, every time you attempt to manage uncertainty and probability, you first have to manage the emotional brain so that it does not hijack the rational brain. It is here that emotion and reason have to harnessed to work together for an effective mind to manage uncertainty. Otherwise, the fear of the unknown will trigger and reason becomes slave to emotion quickly.

New Leadership at the Helm

This trader has to teach his brain a new leadership style for success in trading. There is nothing wrong with his current leadership style applied to business negotiations. He has proven successful in business, family, community, and church life – nearly all the domains that are important to him. The problem is that success in trading is a different animal than success in these domains. It's really a matter of personal growth and whether or not he is motivated to adapt his leadership style to a new domain with different rules. The major renegotiation is his stance toward the management of uncertainty. For him uncertainty has always been something he could control by his cunning, his willingness to engage risk, and his will to win. This formula worked for many years, and still does in the rest of his life – just not in trading.

Now he has to harness even his leadership style for success in trading. Whereas he was always able to control outcome by personal force, he now recognizes that in trading he cannot control outcome. What he can control, he recognizes, is the mind he brings to the performance of execution. The new leader emerges here. Instead of getting the last drop of blood out of a deal, his task is to take profits when targets are hit or when structure begins to break down – rather than forcing his will upon the market gods.

He becomes a steward to his brain and his mind that arises out of it. It is a brain/mind that can be designed (rather than waiting for his ship to come in). He is moving from what became (through experience) an instinctual response to stress – taking control – to a mind that has control over only one thing – the mind that is brought into a particular moment in time to manage performance.

Rather than external leadership, he is now focusing on internal leadership. As useful as the old leadership style was for success in the past, it had to be adapted for success in the world of trading.

Trading required a different kind of leadership for success. Not better or worse than the precepts he brought to trading – just different.

Now he has the tools and skills to see the thief approaching from a distance. He is no longer so easily robbed. The very urge to get the last drop of profit (and not be satisfied till he did) was, in fact, the thief who used to sneak up on him and pick-pocket him. He actually came to wonder how he could have been so blind to have missed it. It was not his IQ and external knowledge that won the day, it was his internal knowledge of what made him tick and learning how to change it that got him past his self-imposed road block and made him a successful trader.

Rande Howell

www.tradersstateofmind.com.

CHAPTER 4 – CAPITAL EXPOSURE VS. PROBABILITY BY JAIME JOHNSON

Everyone likes lower capital exposure trade set-ups because lower capital exposure means lower risk. However, lower capital exposure usually means there is a lower probability your trade will be successful than a trade with higher capital exposure. Higher capital exposure, while higher monetary risk, gives the trade more room to avoid being prematurely stopped out by market noise. I usually trade the end of corrections so before I give examples of capital exposure vs. probability, let's discuss trends and counter trends, aka impulsive and corrective patterns. I am a FOREX trader, so the examples in this article are FOREX examples. However, these trade strategies and theories can be applied to any market in any time frame.

Trading the End of a Correction

There are two things to know about trends or impulsive waves, they tend to unfold in non-overlapping wave patterns and they tend to unfold in the direction of the higher degree timeframe trend. In other words, a Bull impulsive wave in the 60 minute chart is probably unfolding in the same direction as the trend of the higher degree time frame 240 minute chart. See Chart 1, a GBP/JPY 60 minute chart. The rally from the May 12 low to May 12 high unfolded in a non overlapping impulsive pattern so the higher degree time frame trend is probably bullish.

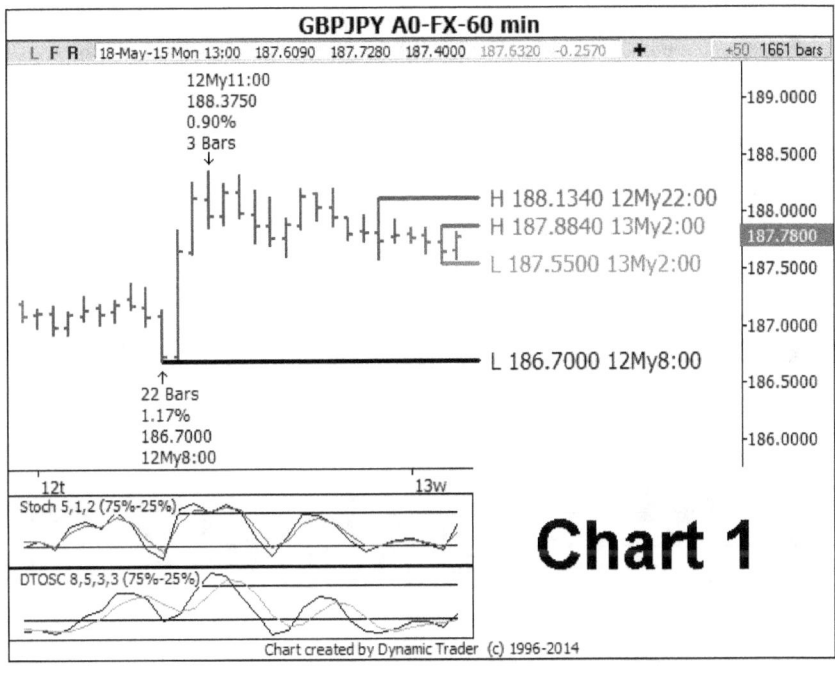

Chart 1

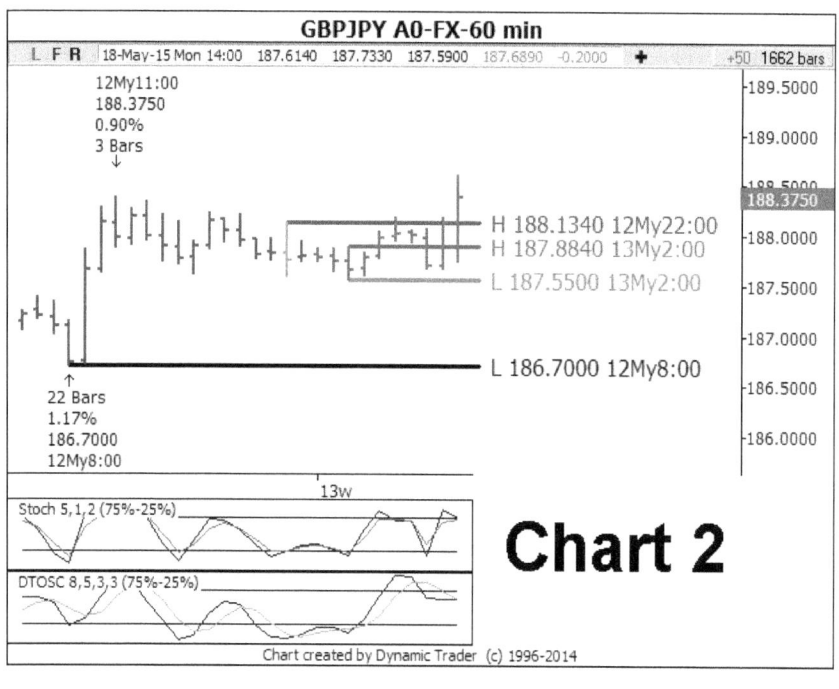

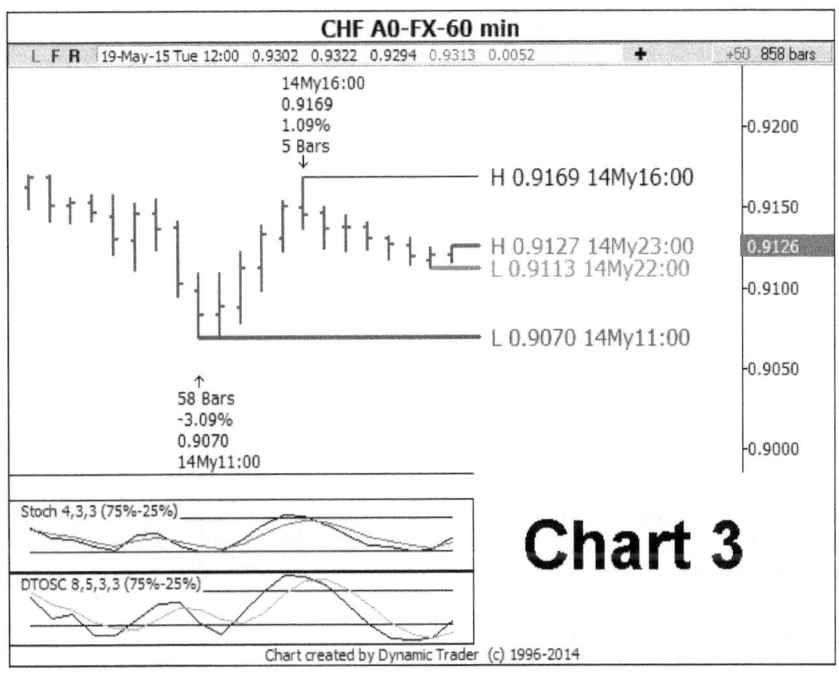

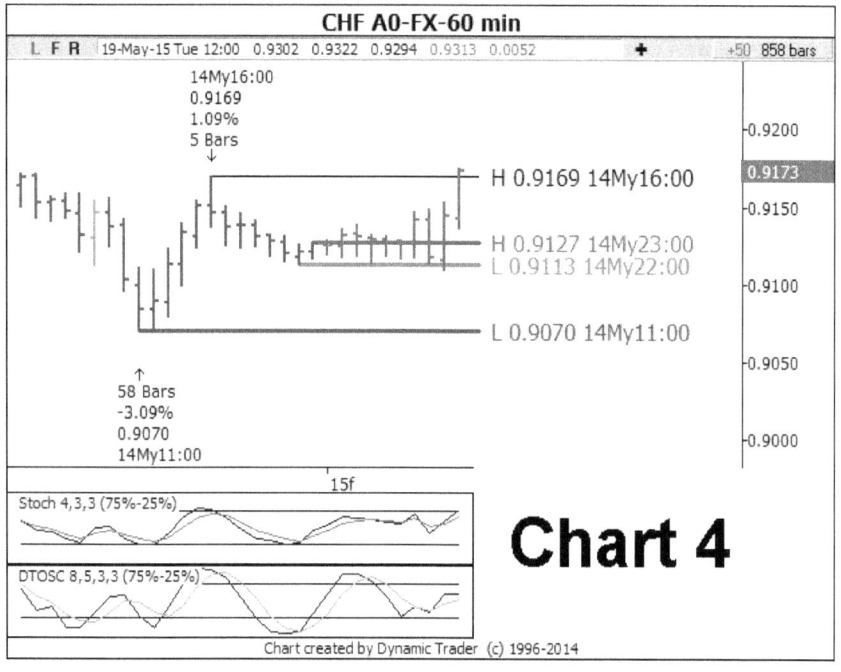

Two important things about countertrends or corrections, they usually unfold in an overlapping wave pattern and they usually unfold in the opposite direction of the higher degree time frame trend direction. See Chart 1 (the decline off the May 12 high has overlapping corrective characteristics). So it is advantageous to learn to get into a trade at or near the end of a correction, in the opposite direction of the correction, which should put you in a trade in the direction of the higher degree time frame trend. The tricky part is knowing when a correction is at or near completion and a good tool for this is to use a dual time frame oscillator trade strategy.

1. Use an oscillator with a setting that correlates well with the swing highs and lows of the market and time frame you are looking at. The DTosc (a proprietary oscillator to the Dynamic Trader Software), the Slow Stochastic and Stochastic RSI are my favorite oscillators.

2. Only trade in the direction of the higher degree time frame oscillator direction. For example, if the 240 minute oscillator is oversold or Bull, only consider long trade set-ups in the 60 minute time frame.

3. In the trade entry time frame, also use an oscillator to help determine the end of the correction, so if the higher degree time frame oscillator is oversold or bull only take long trade set-ups when the trade entry time frame oscillator is oversold or Bull.

Once again go to Chart 1. With the decline off the GBP/JPY May 12 high with corrective characteristics, it is very likely the May 12 high will be exceeded before the May 12 low is taken out. The higher degree time frame 240 minute oscillator is oversold, so long positions may be considered in the 60 minute time frame as long as the 60 minute oscillator is oversold or Bull. Both the 60 minute DTosc and the slow stochastic are Bull. Long positions may be considered for a probable rally to above the May 12 high.

Capital Exposure vs. Probability

Now that we have gone over the basics for a dual time frame trade strategy for the end of a correction, let's discuss capital exposure. The capital exposure of a trade is the value between the entry price and stop-loss price. It is first calculated in pips then it can be translated into monetary value. So why do traders like lower capital exposure trades? Because there is a less monetary risk. However, it is not always the best idea to trade low capital exposure trade set-ups because the probability of the trade being successful is less. Trades with a further stop give the trade more room to work through market noise. So there is a give and take: higher capital exposure = high probability while lower capital exposure = lower probability.

Back to Chart 1. Both the 240 and 60 minute oscillators are BearOS and Bull, respectively, so long positions may be taken. Where the trade will be entered and stop placed determines the capital exposure and probability. I am going to point out a couple of potential places to enter this long trade and a couple of potential places to place the initial protective sell-stop. Potential entries are shown with the blue and green horizontal lines and stop loss places are below the red or black horizontal lines. There are four potential trade set-ups listed below from lower to higher capital exposure.

1. Entering above the green line, placing stop below red line.
2. Entering above the blue line, placing stop below the red line.
3. Entering above the green line, placing stop below the black line.
4. Entering above the blue line, placing stop below the black line

While these four trades set-ups are listed from lower to higher capital exposure, they are also listed by lower to higher probability. However, looking at Chart 2, no matter which trade set-up was taken, they all were successful with the rally above the May 12 high.

What Trade Set-ups Should I Take?

Looking at the first example you are probably saying I should take the lower capital exposure trade set-ups with less risk. Before you decide this let's take a look at Chart 3, a 60 minute USD/CHF chart. The rally off the March 14 low to the 0.9169 swing high has impulsive characteristics followed by a decline with a sideways to down pattern characteristic of a correction. The higher time frame 240 minute oscillator is Bull, the 60 minute DTosc and slow stochastic made Bullish Reversals following the completion of the last 60 minute bar. This is a nice trailing one bar high dual time frame long trade set-up for a potential rally to above the 0.9169 swing high.

With the trailing one bar high trade set-up, once the oscillator makes a BullRev go long above the high of the last completed one bar high, in this case, above 0.9127 (green). If the trade does not get triggered and both the 60 minute and 240M oscillators are still oversold or bull, adjust the entry price to above the last completed 60 minute bar (the entry is being trailed). If this trade is entered, there are two places to put the protective sell-stop, below the last swing low, in this case below 0.9113 (red) or below the March 14 low (blue). A trade below the March 14 low is the only place that voids a corrective decline off the 0.9169 high.

See Chart 4. The long trade was triggered and if you placed the protective sell-stop below the red line for the low capital exposure trade, it would have been stopped out later in the day for a loss followed by a rally to above the 0.9169 swing high confirming the corrective low. However, if you would have placed the stop below the May 14 low, the higher capital exposure, but higher probability trade set-up, the trade was successful. Having the stop further way gave room to the trade for the market noise that would have stopped out the lower capital exposure trade.

So Higher Capital Exposure Trade Set-Ups are Better?

Not necessarily. There are positive and negatives for both trade set-ups. Lower capital exposure trades usually come with lower probability, but higher profit potential. Higher capital exposure trades usually come with higher probability, but lower profit potential. Lower capital exposure trades usually come with many small losses, but the losses can easily be covered with a profit by one successful trade. Higher capital exposure trades usually come with many small profitable trades, but the losses can be very big.

Only you can decide which trade set-ups are good for you. I call a person who should only take higher capital exposure/higher probability trade set-ups a Type 1 trader. Traders who are able to trade lower capital exposure/lower probability trade set-ups are Type 2 traders. While only you can decide which trade set-ups to take, I can help you determine if you are a Type 1 or Type 2 trader. Please check out my free ebook "10 Questions to Determine What Type of Trader You Are: A Prerequisite to Becoming a Successful Trader". It can be downloaded at www.nobsfx.com.

Use a Money Management Plan.

When using a money management plan you should have a maximum amount that can be lost in any trade. While money management is a subject that deserves its own article, I do teach a detailed money management plan in my NoBSFX Trading Course. In a nutshell, equations are used in which you input your capital exposure, max. amount that can be lost, etc. The equation will spit out how many lots or units are allowed to be used in that trade. While this will curb your risk, it usually also curbs profit potential.

Knowing what type of trader you are is just one aspect of being a good trader. You also must always use objective trade entry strategies, always use stop-losses, trade more than one unit and have exit strategies for each unit, use stop-loss adjustment strategies, use a money management plan and most importantly, be disciplined enough to stick to these trade strategies.

If you liked this article, check out my Traders World Online Expo Presentation for further explanation as well as a discussion on the current market position of the EUR/USD. Happy Trading!

Jaime Johnson

www.nobsfxtrading.com

jaime@nobsfxtrading.com

Chapter 5 - New Tools for Trend Analysis and Swing Trading By George Krum

In this brief presentation we will introduce four new and exclusive indicators recently included in OT Signals and our mobile apps. They include the Trend Bars and the Trend Bars Signal indicator, Swing Angles and the Angles SAR indicator.

The Trend Bars indicator is a novel way of displaying the underlying trend by eliminating the noise from random price moves and by sidestepping certain drawbacks associated with traditional charting techniques.

After Japanese candlesticks gained popularity in technical analysis, they were quickly followed by the introduction of additional Japanese charting techniques such as Renko, Kagi, and Heikin-Ashi. Although they all strive to visually improve our perception of the bullish and bearish trends driving markets, they also pose some challenges. Interpreting candlesticks and remembering the myriad of bullish and bearish formations can be demanding. Renko and Kagi lack the element of time, and along with Heikin-ashi suffer from additional problems such as delayed reaction to price changes.

To remedy these problems we've developed the Trend Bars indicator exclusively for OT Signals and our mobile apps. The goal was to create a multipurpose tool that is simple to interpret, yet performs several tasks without cluttering the chart space and without leading to analysis paralysis.

First of all, we were striving for simplicity and clarity. This feature of Trend Bars becomes immediately obvious after we compare it to a candlestick chart, for example (Chart 1A):

While on the daily SPX candlestick chart below it is sometimes difficult to determine the trend and reversal points:

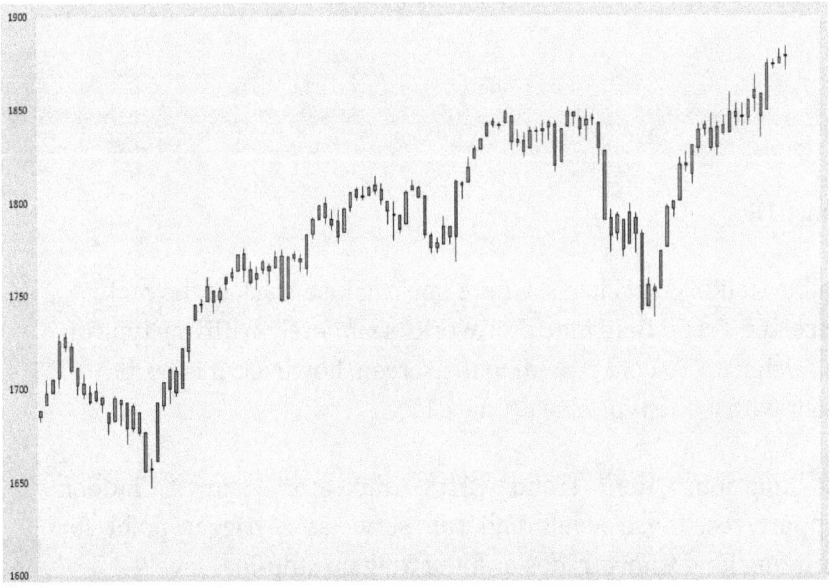

Chart 1A

Trend Bars makes this task much easier. Uptrends are painted in green, and downtrends – in purple (Chart 1B):

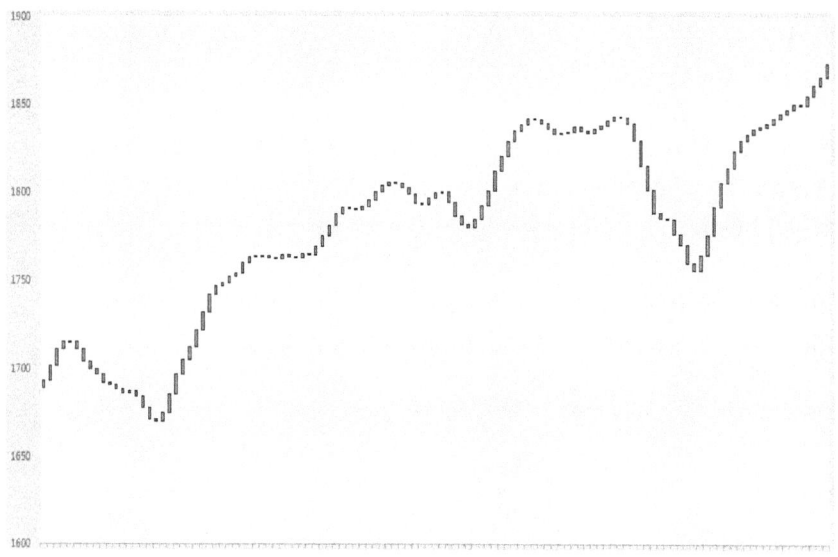

Chart 1B

Unlike Heikin-Ashi charts, where one can lose track of the real price, the Trend Bars indicator works seamlessly with any type of price chart. To avoid crowding the screen, however, it is best to use it with a line type chart (Chart 1C).

In addition, the Trend Bars indicator shows hidden support/resistance levels and can serve as a trigger point for initiating long/short trades or for setting up stop-loss levels.

Another useful property of the Trend Bars indicator is the fact that the bars tend to get longer when the trend gains strength, and shorter when the trend weakens or is about to end. We've incorporated this feature into the Trend Bars Signals indicator which identifies areas where the Trend Bars give a warning that the current trend is weakening. This feature of the Trend Bars indicator is used by the Trend Bars Signal indicator, available exclusively in OT Seasonal (by the time of publication, it may be available in OT Signals as well, check the User Guide for updates). This indicator turns yellow when the Trend Bars narrow, thus issuing an early warning signal that momentum is slowing and a change in trend may be imminent (Chart 1C):

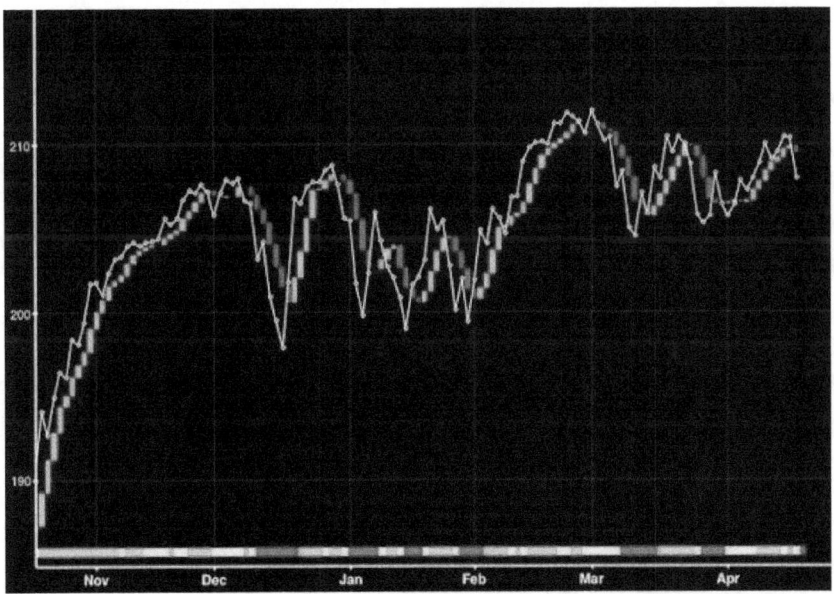

Chart 1C, data courtesy of OT Seasonal.

In summary, the Trend Bars indicator combines elements of momentum detection and trend following, making it an ideal tool for swing and trend traders alike.

The second set of indicators we would like to introduce are Swing Angles and the Swing SAR (stop-and-reverse) indicator. Both indicators are logical extensions of our Swing Time and Swing % indicators, discussed in TradersWorld #57. In a nutshell, the Swing Time Indicator measures key statistics relevant to swing duration (time component), while the Swing % indicator gathers information on key price metrics for a particular instrument (price component).

Combining the price and time component lead to the development of the Swing Angles Indicator. It automatically calculates the correct step (price incremental increase/decrease) for drawing the angles and by default displays the 1 x 1 angles from swing highs and lows. Users, of course, have the ability to select harmonic angles as well. In other words, the Swing Angles Indicator displays the expected path the analyzed security should follow after a new change in trend. Any divergence from that path sends a clear signal that price is deviating from the norm and urgent action may be needed (chart 2):

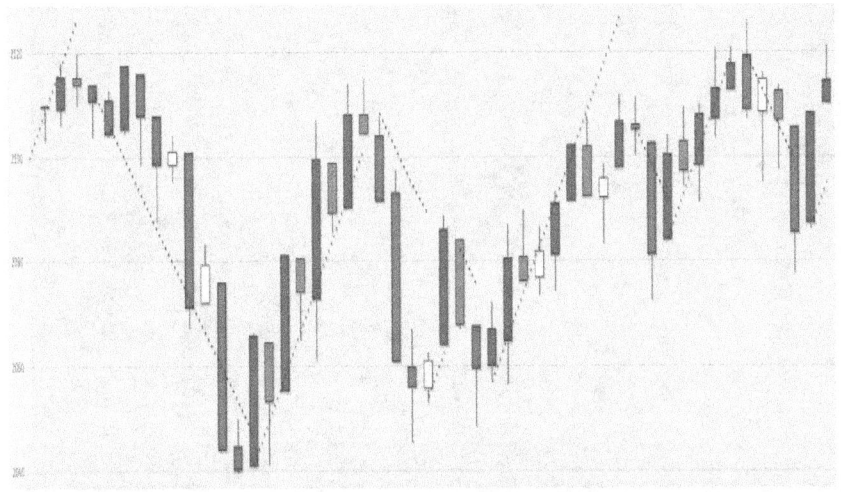

The Angles SAR Indicator, as the name implies, is a stop-and-reverse type indicator based on Swing Angles. Unlike the Swing Angles Indicator, which changes direction from swing highs and lows (as detected by our swing detection algorithm), the SAR indicator changes direction whenever the close crosses above or below an up/down Swing Angle. After this takes place, the SAR indicator will display by default the 1 x 1 angle in the opposite direction. Users, of course, have the ability to display harmonic angles as well (chart 3):

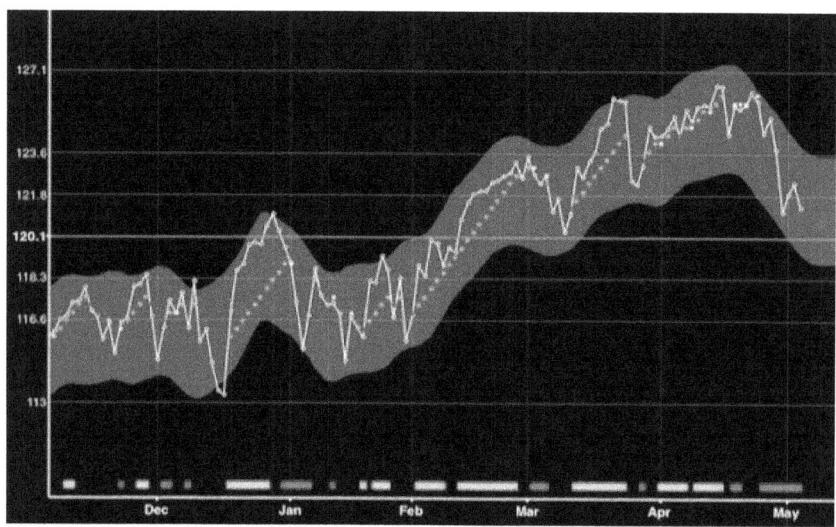

Chart 3

As you can see, the Angles SAR Indicator starts and ends with price breaking above/below the current trend support and resistance levels, and complements the Swing Angles Indicator by introducing another variable for detecting trend changes.

Currently, this indicator is available only in Gann 9, but by the time of publication, or shortly thereafter, should be available in OT Signals as well. You can check the User Guide for availability.

In summary, the Swing Angles Indicator and the Angles SAR Indicator are two indispensable tools for every trader, which will allow you to predict and follow the natural rhythm (rate of vibration, if you will) of individual securities and the whole market, as represented by the broader averages.

Chapter 6 - A Complete Guide To Order Flow Trading Through Volume Price Analysis: The Banks' Forex Secret By Ricardo Menjivar

Enter Chapter Content What you are about to learn will change the way you trade and look at trading forever especially when it comes to the Foreign Exchange Markets. In this chapter you will learn how the banks hide their plan of action through their volume activity by using algorithmic high frequency protocols they have designed to hide their real intent from the Retail Trader. Now, if I have your attention, then don't stop reading because what I am going to show you in the coming pages will finally make you aware of the new truth. A wise man once said the truth will set you free but in this case, the truth will make you money beyond your wildest dreams.

I am excited to share this new state of the art technology that we have created to decode the Market Makers/Banks intent. You will learn that we take fear and doubt away from your decision process before entering the trade. You see we don't use conventional indicators like Moving Averages, MACD, Stochastic, RSI, or others because the banks have counter programmed those outdated indicators and that is why you can't get an edge on the trade. Because of this many of you turn to chart pattern recognition programs that do not work for you either. So do yourself a favor and don't stop reading this chapter or seeing our video. Where we demonstrate how we made over 700 pips with only four (4) pairs.

One of the things that you will discover is that with PhoenixTradingStrategies.com you have reached the finish line. We are the final frontier when it come to Order Flow trading and Volume Price Analysis because we understand it better than anyone.

What Is the Forex Created For?

The Forex is a market created by a network of banks that are in the business of buying and selling currencies. Most banks and retail traders in many cases trade twenty eight (28) pairs that are derived from the eight (8) major currencies which are the following:

USD,EUR,CHF,GBP,JPY,AUD,NZD,CAD.

EUR/USD	EUR/CAD	EUR/CHF	EUR/GBP
EUR/ JPY	EUR/AUD	EUR/NZD	GBP/USD
GBP/CAD	GBP/CHF	GBP/JPY	GBP/AUD
GBP/NZD	CHF/JPY	CHF/CAD	AUD/CHF
NZD/CHF	USD/CHF	AUD/USD	AUD/NZD
AUD/CAD	AUD/JPY	NZD/USD	NZD/CAD

NZD/JPY   USD/CAD   USD/CHF   USD/JPY

Now you and I both know that everyone out there emphasize that you should only trade the majors because that is where most of the volume is traded. There is some merit to that but I will show you that they have a different agenda that does not always apply to the major pairs.

What are the major pairs?

EUR/USD , GBP/USD , AUD/USD , NZD/USD , USD/CHF , USD/JPY , USD/CAD

Currency Portfolio Rebalancing

Currency Portfolio Rebalancing is a theory where the Market Makers/Banks base their decision process for creating their algorithms. The whole purpose of this theory and the protocols are designed around managing their risk and exposure with currencies in the market. You see the banks cannot have too much exposure of one particular currency and must maintain a balance between the (8) eight major currencies. So they will buy and sell currencies all day long to manage their risk. Retail traders don't think about this because they get too caught up in other information that doesn't matter.

Currency Portfolio Rebalancing is the idea that money is in continuous motion but that there is a balance that must be maintained between the portfolio of the eight (8) major pairs. While some currencies are trading within a specific frequency of balance others are taken out of balance and then brought back into balance. The example below portrays this concept.

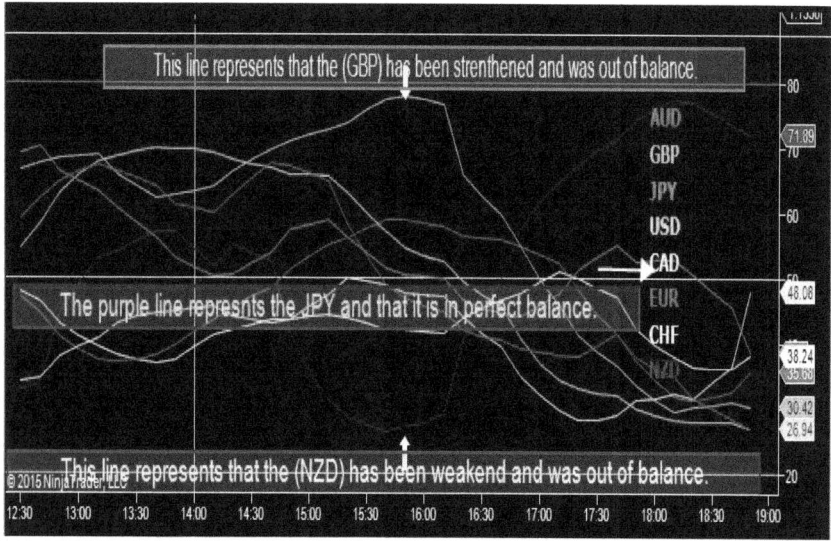

The example above shows how each individual currency is trading against the other seven (7) currencies. It depicts how money is in continuous motion by showing that no currency can trade out of balance for too long without it being brought back into balance. Example the Orange line represents the (GBP) British Pound and shows how it had been trading at frequency of strength before being weakened and brought back into balance. The same thing happened to the (NZD) the blue line which was weakened against all seven (7) other currencies and then traded back into balance for the portfolio of (8) eight currencies. The Purple line represent the (JPY) Japanese Yen that was trading in the middle and in perfect balance. This showed that there was no particular interest by the Market Makers to take it out of balance.

In theory it seems logical but how do you apply it in the real trade. Good question and we will get to how you apply it in the live edge of the market later.

Phoenix FX Proprietary Volume Indicator

Let's talk about volume in the FX Market. Reality is that there is no centralized exchange for Forex and that is why you cannot quantify the real volume that the Banks/Market Makers are actually trading. This has been a way to keep the retail trader in the dark. So we have created a proprietary volume indicator that will help the retail trader decode their order flow by synthetically creating volume that can be interpreted and show the degree of interest (EMOTION) that the banks have in rebalancing their risk at certain price levels. We are able to isolate buying and selling volume numerically per bar per time frame. So for example if you are on the (15) fifteen minute time frame. This indicator will show how many millions they are selling and buying in the same candle giving you the depth of the market per candle that you could never see before.

As we continue you will discover that our volume indicator is better than anything that you have ever used to define order flow because it is easy to interpret and can tell you if that candle is really bullish with bullish volume or is really a bullish candle with bearish volume. Intriguing question isn't it?

In the example below you will see how we identify all the volume in the candle that we tagged with a white arrow. Just that one candle had a total of 429.8 million that was quoted in that one bullish green candle that moved a total of 32 pips. More importantly is that within that candle we were able to isolate in panel (2) two, the buying and selling volume that was quoted inside that bar. Showing the real emotion that drove the candle to go long. This has never really been seen before by the Retail Forex Trader. Now imagine if you knew when it mattered to look at the volume and understand that they were rebalancing their risk by offsetting their short positions before driving the trade long the way they did here. You will see later how valuable this information is to your decision process because our software alerts you when you should be analyzing the volume per candlestick because the market makers/banks have decided to execute their plan of action at a particular price level.

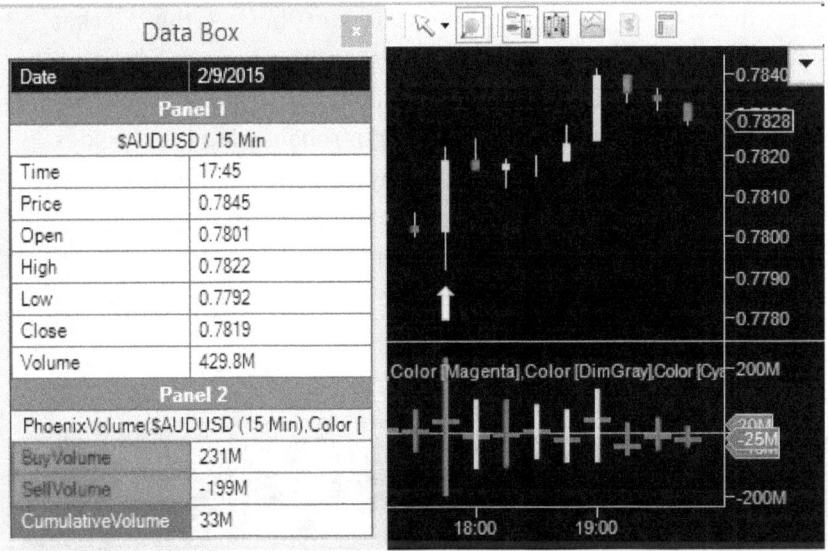

In the example above you see the volume bars and a line that runs in the middle which is the mean. The to the far left that candle looks like a shooting star and is a great example of a bearish candle with bullish volume because the little gray line on the red volume bar shows that the volume settled with a bullish outcome. So yes interpreting volume does matter at certain price levels where they have decided to trade away from.

What are the Phoenix Power Dots?

Why is it that retail traders the last to know before volume and momentum are driven into a currency pair. Why can't that information become more noticeable to the human eye. That is question that all traders ask themselves because they lack the right information to plan their trade out before the Market Makers/Banks decide to move the market. The Power Dots is an algorithmic piece of art that we created to identify when the Market Makers/Banks are about to begin rebalancing their trades around a specific price level where they had chosen to offset their short orders in order to drive the trade long. The example below shows a graphic display of that powerful information that will alert you hours in advance so you can plan your entry, stop loss and even price target without fear.

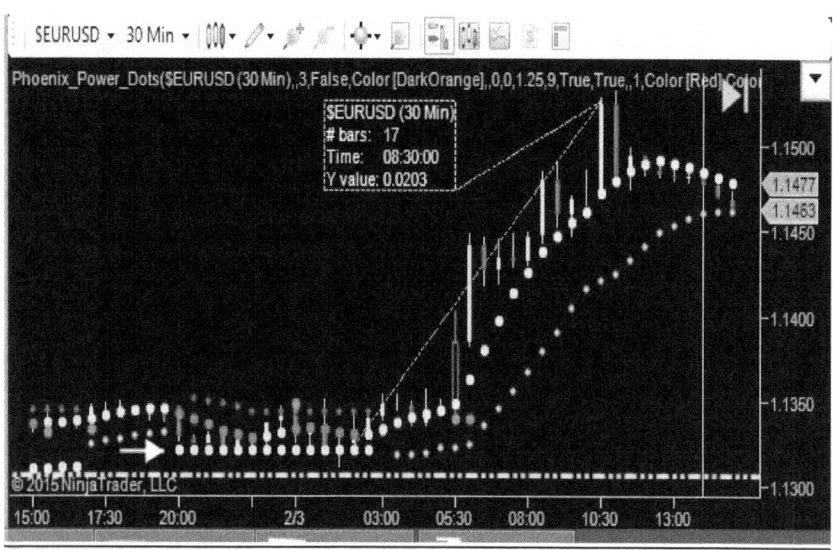

The Gold Dots are the Phoenix Power Dots. In this example above you can clearly see how in the thirty (30) minute time frame they plotted at 20:00 hours above the green line which is another price level that plotted in a higher time frame isolating the price level that the banks refused to break support because if they did they would also trigger other algorithms from other banks that would create a selling frenzy instead of driving it long the way they planned for hours while they offset their short positions. And where you see the Power Dots form is exactly where the banks do a lot of high frequency trading so when you combine the Phoenix Volume with it you can see how desperate they are per candle to rebalance their orders but never trade below the Power Dots because their intent here was always to go long 200 pips to the upside. Now think about this the Power Dots began to form five (5) hours before the trade went long. So you had a five (5) hour window to determine your entry, stop loss and take profit target.

This is powerful information that I am sharing with you and you will appreciate it even more when you see our video and how we made over 700 pips in one night with 4 trades using this software.

In this example below we combine all the indicators together to tell you the story. You can see in the data box on the left the Power Dots formed at 1.1320 which was right above 1.1306 where the green line was plotted. So the price of 1.1320 was established by the Market Makers as the price level that they were going to aggressively rebalance their short positions. The first Gold Power Dot shows the amount of volume that they were desperate to sell. In Panel 2 on the Data box you can see that they were desperate to offset -292 Million on the sell side against 231 Million on the buy side. Leaving -60 Million that they could not offset in that candle. So you see this price level is where they were going to do all their high frequency trading to get out of their short positions before driving this trade long. Thus, the reason why we call this Order Flow Trading with Volume Price Analysis.

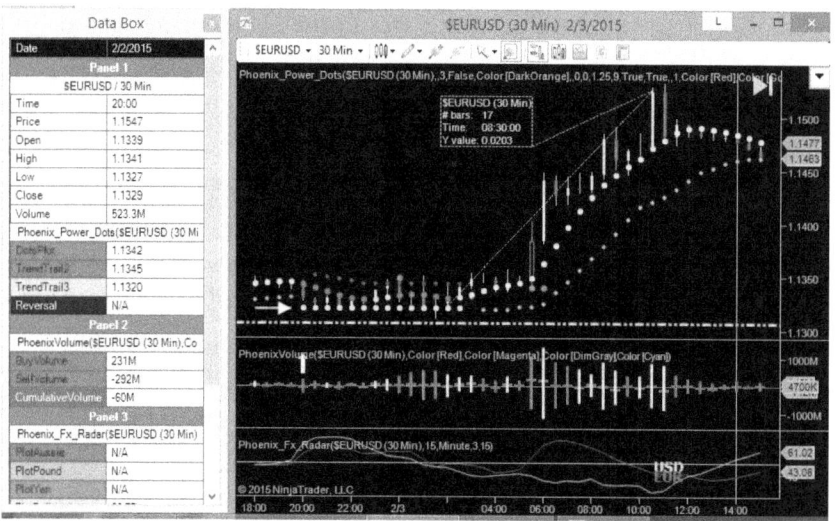

So when you see the combination of facts and numbers; is it fair to say that they have counter programmed candlesticks because without this software alerting you and calculating all this information for you to define and decode the Market Makers/Banks intent you would have never thought that they were really intending to drive the trade long over 200 pips from that support level.

Finally we put you in control of the trade by creating a Market Analyzer that will alert you when the Gold Power Dots form in any of the 28 currency pairs that you prefer to trade. This is the icing on the cake because it reduces your analysis time to when you should be looking at the market not being a slave to it. Oh yeah, this baby will take you to the promise land. You can program it to alert you when it says Analyze Me. This tells you that Power Dots have formed at certain Price Levels that are of special interest to the Banks. You can see below that there are five (5) Currency Pairs and one (1) the E-Mini Nasdaq that are in play. This takes your focus to what the banks want to manipulate not what you think is going to happen. So if you are ready to trade the right way, you will want to add this suite of indicators to your arsenal.

Instrument	15	Current	Congestion	WideBar	Phoenix_Power_	Price to Congesti
NQ 03-15					Analyze Me	
YM 03-15			Congestion			Trade With Me
GC 04-15						
$AUDJPY					Analyze Me	
$AUDUSD			Congestion		Analyze Me	
$CADJPY			Congestion			Trade With Me
$EURAUD						
$EURGBP						
$EURJPY						
$EURNZD						
$EURUSD						
$GBPAUD						
$GBPCAD						
$GBPJPY						
$GBPNZD					Analyze Me	
$GBPUSD			Congestion			Trade With Me
$NZDUSD					Analyze Me	
$USDCAD						
$USDJPY					Analyze Me	

Market Analyzer

Conclusion

Whatever you decide to do? I want to wish you the very best in your journey to Trading the Forex Markets. I hope that in this journey you choose PhoenixTradingStrategies.com as your guide to staying (10) steps ahead of the Banks.

CHAPTER 7 - THE TREND CONTINUATION TRADE BY JOHN MATTESON

If you have been trading for any length of time, you are probably familiar with the concepts of support and resistance. Typically, you want to be a buyer in support or a seller in resistance. For many traders, this forms the core of their trading plan. Finding levels of support and resistance can be a bit of a subjective pursuit, but however one derives their support and resistance levels, their plan is typically to buy at their support levels and sell at their resistance levels.

The majority of the time, support levels act as support and resistance levels tend to act as resistance, but they are not 100%. Sometimes, markets like to trend. If a trend has developed, the markets may choose to simply go through a given support or resistance level. In other words, about 1/3 of the time, markets like to trend. In the case of a trending market, support will not act as support nor will resistance act as resistance. During these trending days, the trader buying support and selling resistance may experience many losing trades and potentially frustration.

There is, however, a way that a trader of support and resistance levels can recognize a market that wants to trend and potentially jump aboard that trend using what I call a trend continuation trade. What follows are the steps we use at MTPredictor to identify when a trend may develop or continue.

Step 1 – Finding Support and Resistance

First, we need to identify our levels of support and resistance. To do this, I will use the MTPredictor decision point levels. These are leading indicators that will be on the chart in advance of the market potentially reaching those levels. (See chart 1) We call these decision points because the market needs to make a decision at these levels. Typically, these levels will act as support and resistance about two thirds of the time. But, about one third of the time, the market will go through these levels and continue to trend. In other words, the decision the market makes at these levels will be to continue the current trend rather than act as support or resistance.

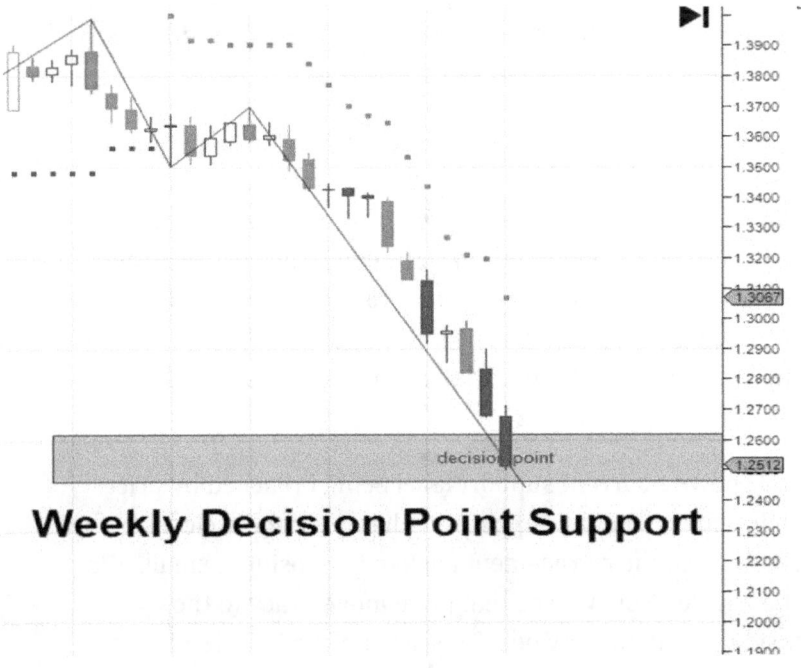

Chart 1.

These decision point levels are generated from a larger degree time frame. For instance, if you plan to trade from a three minute or five minute chart, you would go to the fifteen minute chart and add the DP support and resistance levels on to the chart. If you trade from a daily chart, you will use the weekly chart to map out larger degree support and resistance levels. Whatever time frame you choose to to look for your trade entries, you will look to the chart that is about three to five times greater to add your support and resistance levels.

Step 2. The Setup

Once you have identified your support and resistance levels on your larger time frame, you can drop down to your trading time frame and wait for a potential setup.

What we will be looking for is a move in price into one of our DP support or resistance levels. Remember, two thirds of the time, these levels will act as support or resistance. What we want to see is if price will go through the level, breaking the level, and then potentially retrace. Once price has retraced, we will wait and see if the new high or low is broken. If it is, there is a high probability that the trend will continue and the support or resistance level will be broken. (see chart 2)

Chart 2 shows a current support level being breached by price which has moved below support and has two candle closes below the level. Next, the retracement back to the upside is small. We call it a wiggle. Now we see that price moves back to the downside, taking the low out. This sets up our Decision Point, trend continuation trade.

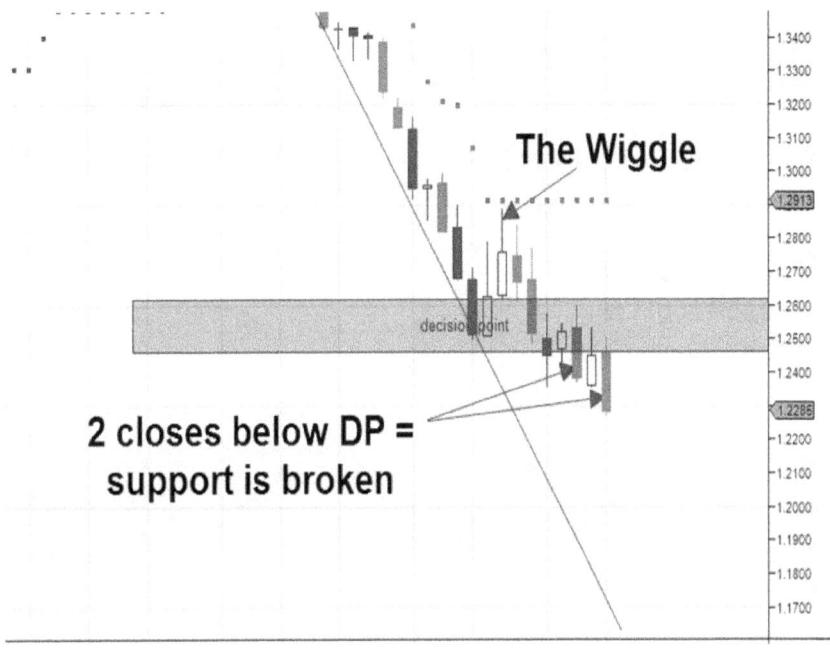

The Wiggle

2 closes below DP = support is broken

decision point

Chart 2.

Part 3. Executing the Trade

Once price has gone through our DP level, we wait for at least two candle closes below the level to confirm the level is indeed broken. We will make note of the lowest low at this point. If price begins to retrace, we will look for a break of the lowest low as our entry point. Once the retracement is finished and price begins to decline, we will use this retracement high to set our protective stop above. (see chart 3)

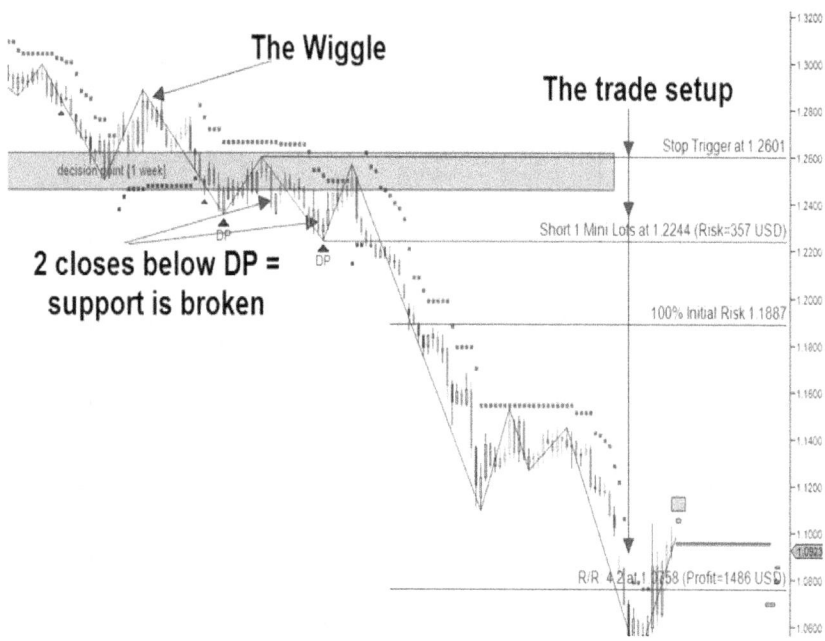

Chart 3.

We will look for a target that is at least twice our initial risk. This target may be a lower decision point level, average true range or any other logical price target level. We can also look to trail a stop using our ATR trailing stop indicator.

I would recommend not risking more than 2% of your trading capital for this. You may want to start with less. The size of your position should be based on your risk tolerance and the size of the stop required. So, for instance, if you want to risk 2% on your $20,000 of risk capital, this means your maximum risk will be $400. Let's say the stop required is 2 points for a setup in the ES (S&P emini). With a stop of 2 points (each point is worth $50) and

$400 to risk, this means you can trade a maximum of 4 contracts. This ensures you are keeping your risk small and controlled while your rewards will be larger. This will mean that you won't have to be highly accurate in terms of your win percentage in order to be profitable. It also means that you will be controlling the only thing you can – your initial risk.

As you will see, markets tend to trend only about one third of the time. Recognizing this setup will give you an edge on these days when a trend develops and continues through support and resistance. Once you recognize this pattern, you will know not to employ trades that take advantage of fading support but rather use trend type trade strategies.

Part 4. An Additional Trend Continuation Setup

There is another trend continuation setup that takes advantage of a tendency in Elliott wave patterns. In this case, after the completion of a 5 wave sequence, chart 4 shows a completed 5 wave sequence up. Price has stopped at the typical wave 5 target. At this point we anticipate that the market will correct back to the wave 4 decision point. If this wave 4 decision point holds as support then the trend, which was up prior, should continue up. If, however, the wave 4 DP is broken to the downside, then the tendency will be that the market will wipe out the entire prior 5 wave sequence up to the downside. If we see that the wave 4 DP gives way, then we will take a DP off of the start of the wave 1 swing low. This gives us our target for this setup.

So, let's set this trade up. If price approaches our wave 4 DP and begins to break through the level, we will look to go short 1 or 2 ticks below the lowest bar close low below the DP level (see chart 5). Typically, there will be an area of consolidation around the DP area. This will provide us with a place to put a protective stop behind. Again, we want to make sure that our reward will be at least twice our initial risk from the entry to the wave 1 DP target.

You can see in the example that we have taken care of the entry, stop, initial target and correct position size in advance of executing the trade. If we lose, we will lose small while the wins will be larger. These trades set up in any liquid market and time frame. You can use any chart type you like from Renko and Range bars to tick and time based charts.

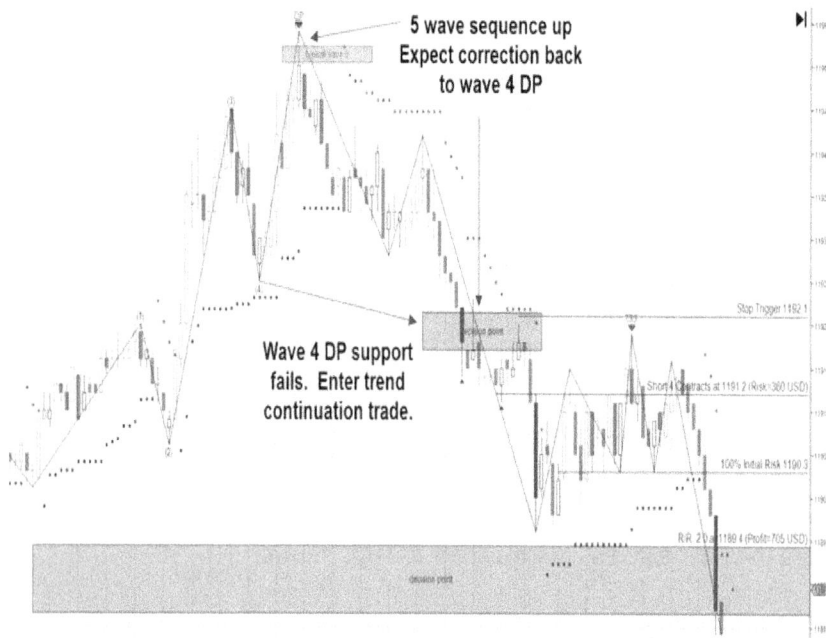

Chart 4.

Wrapping Up

About two thirds of the time, markets will rally off support levels and sell off from resistance levels. One third of the time, however, the markets will trend through these levels. There is a way to take advantage of the times when support fails to act as support and resistance fails to act as resistance. It is called a decision point continuation trade. In other words, we are taking advantage of the instances when the market makes the decision to continue a trend. First, we make sure the level has been broken. The evidence will be seen once we have 2 bar closes below our larger degree DP support or 2 bar closes above our larger degree DP resistance levels. We can then set up a low risk, high reward trade setup to take advantage of this tendency.

We can also look for a completed 5 wave sequence that has corrected to the wave 4 DP. We will watch to see if this level acts as support/resistance. If it fails to act as support or resistance, we will look for price to continue the new trend and erase the prior 5 wave sequence. Our target will be a decision point taken from the start of the wave 1 swing low.

Hopefully, this will give you a framework in which to understand the context when support and resistance fail and instead the market continues the trend. This framework will then allow you to take advantage of these times and enable you to enter the trend with a low risk, high reward setup that will put you back on the right side of the market.

For more info about this setup and the other advanced trade setups we use at MTPredictor, check out our website at http://www.mtpredictor.us

Chapter 8 - Trading with TurnSignal-Better Entries and Better Exits by Jim Shane

Enter Chapter Content Trading is hard. It requires a serious dedication of your time, money and effort along with a strong sense of discipline and focus to be successful.

So what is the best way to trade? This is a very personal question for each individual trader to answer so, there is no simple solution. Every trader has attended webinars, read articles and even tried software to help them make sense of the markets. Since each trader has been through a different set of experiences, everyone sees the markets differently. Our presentation of TurnSignal and the TurnSignal indicators will show you how you can use our indicators to see what's going on in the market at the moment that you are deciding to enter or exit a trade. We think using TurnSignal will give you the information you need to make better entries and better exits.

Trading with TurnSignal can be a solution for almost any style of trading. Our indicators will overlay the charts created by NinjaTrader, eSignal and TradeStation and Multicharts. TurnSignal indicators can be used on any market and in any timeframe and provide a view of market movement which allows you to quickly identify current market conditions, allowing you to make better entries and better exits.

As an example, below are two images of the same candlestick chart, the first with no indicators and the second enhanced by overlaying six separate TurnSignal indicators at the same time. Clearly the information provided by the indicators makes it easier to find direction and momentum in the market movement.

In conclusion, there are as many ways to trade as there are traders in the world. Using indicators to identify significant moments in market movement, combine events to create executions, develop strategies to back test ideas and even to automate these ideas to let the software do the work, are all possible in today's modern trading world. The TurnSignal indicators are all callable for use in strategy development and automation on all of our platforms. There is also a set of alerts, already available for TurnSignal for NinjaTrader. With TurnSignal, you can see immediately what's happening on the chart in front of you, so you can make better entries and better exits.

You can visit TurnSignal's website at www.turnsignal.biz

CHAPTER 9 – THE SECRETS OF SAFE PROFITABLE DAY TRADING BY DAVID HACKBART

Enter Chapter Content. How would you like to DOUBLE your Income simply by working 1 more hour per day?

Safe Day Trading Legal Disclaimer

and its subsidiaries and all "affiliated" individuals assume no responsibilities for your trading and investment results.

Hello and welcome to the Secrets of Safe Day Trading

I am going to go over some very important information for your financial future

So please pay attention

I know your time is valuable - and it is soon to be even more valuable once you learn the secrets of Safe Day Trading.

How would you like to DOUBLE your Income simply by working 1 more hour per day?

You get to pick the hour and the place.

THAT's Right: by trading just one hour per day you can easily make $300 - $500 per hour:

But only if you have the right training!

Yes You Too Can Learn To Trade The Market:

The most powerful & profitable skill you will ever learn for your future and your freedom.

Others are doing it right now, today - Why Not You?
www.SafeDayTrading.org

You're here for a reason: This can help you like it has so many before you

I believe this program is what you have been searching for. Why? Because I know it is exactly what I was searching for, for over 20 years.

This Safe Day Trading system is priceless when you look at how it can transform your life.

It could quickly catapult you to the top 10% money earners in the world if you just take this system and apply it, follow the rules with some degree of discipline just like it has done for so many of our students.

It can happen for you very quickly if you just take our advice and follow the Safe Day Trading Secret Success formula:

Training from SafeDayTrading + Practice + Discipline to follow the rules + Belief + Action = SUCCESS!!!

I want to do everything I can to help you get it, and get IT in a BIG profitable way!

Four Key components for effective short term trading

1. You need to have a trading system that works and is duplicable

a. Safe Day Trading has proven success allowing a very high percentage of students reach their goals of significant extra money daily.

2. You have to have time to learn the program, to practice the process and then when you are ready to trade live and make life changing money.

a. The program is delivered via a membership site – so you access the content when you have the time to relax and absorb the material

b. You will have access for a full year so you can repeat any lessons or videos as many times as you need

c. Now the market is able to be traded 24 hours per day 5 days a week so you will need to find an hour or 2 that works for you.

3. You need to have some capital to invest in yourself.

a. To open your brokerage account you will need at least $500. Obviously more would be better. Most people start with between $5,000 and $10,000 in their trading account. This is your money just like money in your bank. (You pick the brokerage that works for you we will give you a few suggestions)

b. The cost for the Safe Day Trading program is only $329 which gives you 24 x 7 access to the award winning Safe Day Trading membership site.

i. Over 300 pages of written instruction

ii. Over 85 videos of instruction and live trading recordings

iii. Over 50 podcasts

iv. Email support

c. There is private coaching available for those who wish to learn faster or find their learning style is best served by someone providing live feedback

i. Online coaching

ii. Live coaching

4. Multiple streams of income possible:

a. Trade Futures & Commodities like oil, Gold, Silver, Corn, Wheat, natural gas

b. Trade Stocks and Stock Options like Facebook, Netflix, Apple, Microsoft, Bank of America, Tesla, First Solar, Priceline, Amazon, Chase, Pfizer, GE, Kraft, Home Depot etc.

c. Trade Forex, US dollar, Japanese Yen, the Euro, Swiss franc,

d. Wealth Strategies using a portion of your trading income to invest in other safe growth instruments.

e. We also have a very lucrative affiliate program where you can earn by helping others.

Any business venture worth pursuing in needs to have a few components to insure success

1. An expanding market with growth potential:

2. The right timing:

3. Proper income leverage:

4. Minimal dependence on others for your own success:

5. Limited Risk:

6. A simple to learn and effective system to implement to make money:

7. An Entry price that is affordable:

Ok let's talk about those points

1. An expanding market with growth potential:

a. There is no turning back. Over 3 trillion dollars are traded daily and will always continue.

b. Its worldwide and you can trade 24 hours per day

c. You can make money if the market is moving up or moving down.

2. The right timing –

a. There has never been a better time to learn to trade the market.

b. The internet truly levels the playing field

c. Brokerage fees and commissions are at an all-time low. 15 years ago people were paying $20 - $50 fees per trade now its only $5 - $7 per trade.

d. Huge demographic of people who want and need an opportunity to make and grow money for their retirement

3. Proper income leverage:

a. It does not get any better than this. Think about trading options where you control hundreds of stocks of top companies for pennies on the dollar and you can gain 200% and more on your money in 20 minutes or less

b. Or trading oil where you can make $1,000 real money per day for each dollar that oil moves. All you need in your account is $5,000.

4. Limited Risk:

a. When you learn to trade from Safe Day Trading you will be given the iron clad rules to follow that will keep you from losing your shirt or any other article of clothing.

b. The most you should lose on any one trade is $30 - $50 when you follow the rules.

c. You should be right over 70% of the time

d. When you are right you should be making $100 - $200 per trade.

e. The key is you simply follow the rules.

5. Minimal dependence on others for your success:

a. Nothing beats day trading for this

b. You need no employees, no down-line, you don't even need customers

c. You are not waiting on anyone to get things done for you to make money.

6. A simple to learn and effective system to implement to make money

a. with the safe day trading program you will be armed with the techniques and strategies that work

b. Most students are making $200 - $500 per day within the first 2 months and it only grows from there.

7. Entry price that is affordable

a. Safe Day Trading membership is only $329 for complete 24 x 7 access for an entire year.

I hope it is becoming very clear for you: Safe Day Trading is the best avenue for anyone to get to the next income level.

Let me be clear: Safe Day Trading is not a Get Rich Quick Proposition; IT IS however a fantastic means to get rich!

If you want to make a huge difference in your financial future I hope you have reached the conclusion that Learning to Trade is the most powerful and Profitable skill you could ever learn.

If you have not reached that conclusion for yourself by now there are only a couple reasons you could have.

1. You don't feel confident that you would be able to trade the market. You don't have the experience or the training to pick the right trades. You have never traded stocks or anything before.

a. Well fear no more:

i. Safe Day Trading provides the answer for you. We show you step by step. From setting up your platform to making the trade and collecting the money.

ii. We will show you what to trade, when to trade, and just as important when not to trade

iii. We will show you what to look for to locate the ideal trades

2. You are worried about risking huge amounts of money in the market

a. Fear no more

i. Safe Day Trading prides itself on insisting that you limit your risk

ii. We don't want you to risk more than $30 or $50 on any one trade

iii. And we show you how to get into trades that should reward you from $50 to $200 per trade.

iv. You are in and out of trades in anywhere from 2 minutes to 30 minutes.

v. We insist that you paper trade for long enough period of time until you are consistently profitable before you ever go live and risk real money.

vi. Follow our instructions and maintain your discipline to the rules and you can't help but be profitable

What would you do if you knew you could be making $1,000 – $5,000 per week working just 1 – 2 hours per day, And you could learn this skill on your own time? Isn't it time you found out?

A few questions that you need to answer:

Do You want to do this?

Do you want this kind of life?

Can You do this?

Of Course YOU Can.

• After talking to the students who have gone before you from all walks of life, the answer is if I can learn this and if they could all learn this, then for sure you can also do this.

• And do it very well.

• We keep the learning process simple and on Your time schedule

• That's why our student success level is so high.

It doesn't matter what your background is: factory worker, farmer, teacher, construction worker, white collar, blue collar, house wife etc.

It doesn't matter what your educational background is: high school, trade school, college degree.

You can do this because of the simplicity of the course and how you will be taught step by step from opening your own brokerage account to placing your trades to make REAL money!

Learn to read the charts with pin point accuracy.

The person who can accurately predict direction will make consistent money with short term trading. It is our objective to show you how to do just that. Please understand that to predict direction long term – even a month out is a crap shoot. But to predict direction in the next 10 minutes – yes you too can learn to do just that. We will show you how. You can make money no matter which direction the market moves... Up or down or sideways – you win.

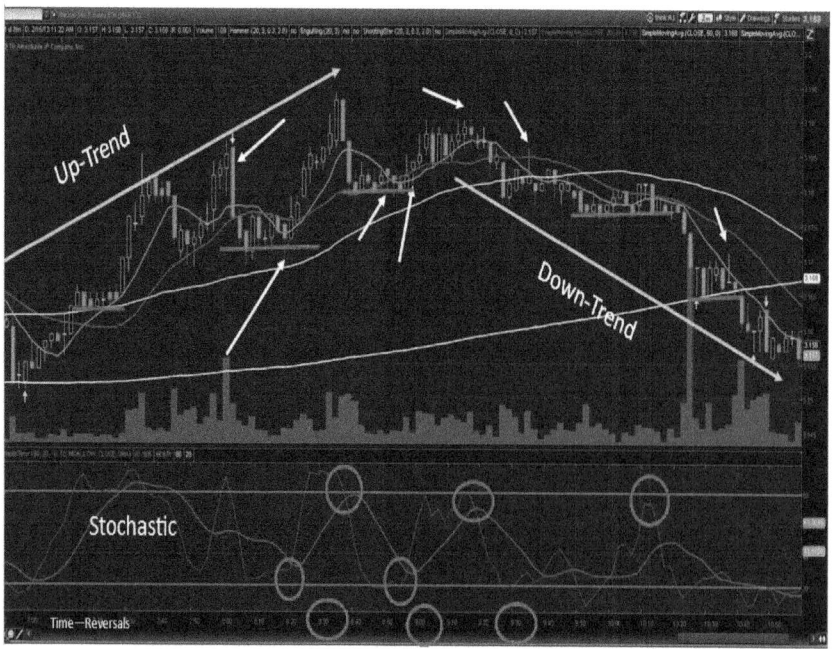

What's included inside Safe Day Trading?

Go to this video to see what's all included in your Safe Day Trading Membership ...

• Youtube.com/SafeDayTrading https://youtu.be/d218cIlf2O0

I'll tell you something that's a sure bet.

• If what you're doing now isn't producing the kind of profits you want, it surely won't do any better in the future.

• Today can be the day that you leverage your time to learn the most powerful skill on the planet and Learn Safe Day Trading.

The Safe Day Trading Program is worth $2,500 all day long but we have it priced significantly less.

Because we want to eliminate any barrier We are offering a Special World Expo price of

Of Less than $500.

We Are Here To Help You – Go to www.SafeDayTrading.org

Chapter 10 - Trading Social Media Sentiment Cycles by Lars von Thienen

Enter Chapter Content. How Social Media Sentiment was able to predict the largest upswing in EUR/USD since 2 years

Back in 1949, investing legend Benjamin Graham eloquently characterized the cyclical nature of financial markets in his book "The Intelligent Investor":

"The market is a pendulum that forever swings between unsustainable optimism and unjustified pessimism."

Today, the emerging field of social media sentiment datasets supports Graham's point of view, providing a strong empirical foundation for the overreaction bias that is often the driving factor in cyclical markets.

Normally, social mood waxes and wanes positively and negatively in the form of dynamic cycles. Social mood refers to a feeling, emotion or attitude about something, and, of course, it can have a range of values. Whenever mood is related to corporations or the economy, the character of events will unfold in the related financial assets. Fear and despondency represents one extreme, while thrill and euphoria represents the other end of the spectrum. (See Chart 1)

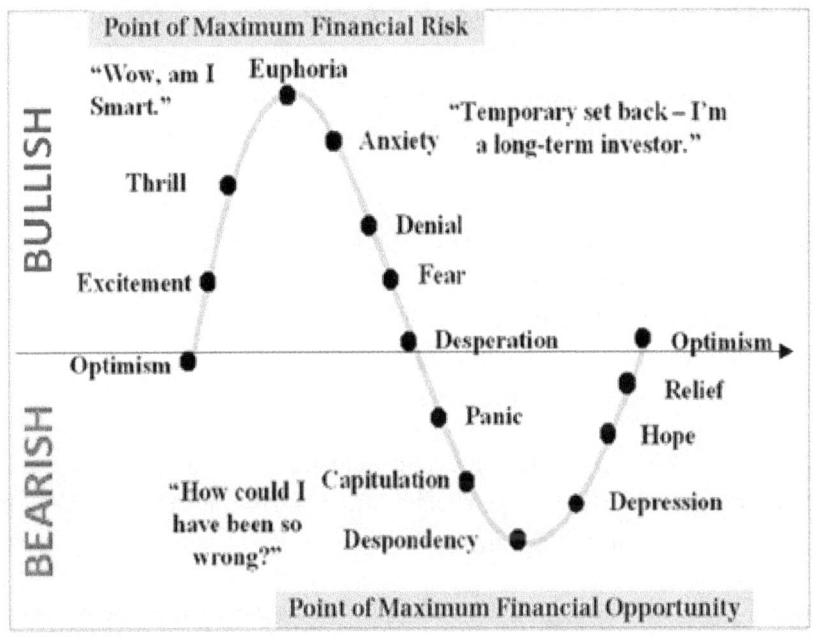

Chart 1: Market pendulum that forever swings between bullish and bearish extremes

Cycles are the important structure here because sentiment does not jump rapidly from one state to another. A change of mood requires time; therefore, sentiment moves in dynamic cycles or waves. This is a similar process to changes in air temperature: the outside temperature does not jump from one state to another. Therefore, the challenge is to spot and predict the extreme turning points called "Maximum Financial Risk" (Euphoria) and "Maximum Financial Opportunity" (Panic/Despondency).

The fascinating aspects of market cyclicality is that the average investor badly underperforms across the board because he or she is prone to chasing performance near market tops and panicking near market bottoms. For this reason, an effective measure of sentiment may be of significant value in identifying the "hot-spots" of maximum financial risk or opportunity within the dominant sentiment cycle.

Consequently, if you have data sets that provide raw social "mood" information related to financial assets on the one hand, and on the other hand have cyclic tools that are able to decipher and track dominant cycles, you have the toolset needed to predict and forecast sentiment "hot-spots".

To underpin the importance on cyclic analysis of social media sentiment, we will review a real case example from March 2015 on the EUR/USD currency pair.

The EUR/USD currency pair traded at 1.081 on March 20th 2015 after pausing a multi-year downtrend for some days (see Chart 2). At this point, it is of major importance to know whether this is just a pause in the overall downtrend and whether one would expect the currency pair to resume going down or to expect a major turnaround. At such times, sentiment cycles can guide the process.

Situation 20th March:
Long downtrend for EURUSD.
Sentiment Cycles issued a
clear call...

↑20. March

^EURUSD Day1 [Replay]

^EURUSD | 2/2/2015 12:00:00 AM | Close: 1.13407 | Bar: 2433 | Y: 1.1... 1:41:15 AM

Chart 2: EUR/USD on March 20th 2015

First, we need raw mood information about EUR/USD.
PsychSignal is a company which provides social sentiment
information derived from internet chatter
(www.psychsignal.com). At every second in every corner of the
Internet, millions of people are expressing their emotions. In this
context, PsychSignal listens to the crowd's mood and builds
bullish/bearish sentiment data clustered according to financial
assets. Such bullish/bearish data is available on their website, on

Quandl or directly accessible via the WhenToTrade Charting and Cycles platform.

Chart 3 shows the composite bullish/bearish sentiment value plotted on a chart in the upper panel (grey). We smoothed the noisy raw data shown by the red line.

In addition, we did run our cycle detection algorithms on the composite social sentiment score. The WhenToTrade ("WTT") platform has an integrated cycle detection algorithm and can decipher the underlying dominant cycle. WTT provides a Dynamic Cycle Explorer toolset that is designed specifically to detect and track cycles that do not stay static in real-time data sets. This is very important because we do not want to detect static cycles that fit to the past – we need cycles that can explain the past but focus more on staying in sync with current market characteristics.

The detected dominant cycle of 208 days is also shown in the lower panel on the chart. The cycle was detected automatically. The turns have been mapped with red and green arrows against the raw sentiment in the upper panel.

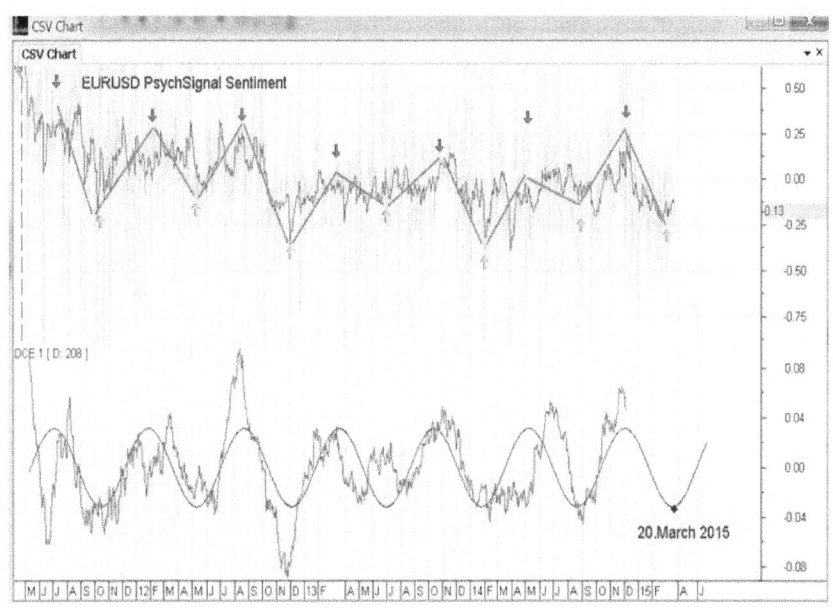

Chart 3: PsychSignal EUR/USD Bullish/Bearish Social Media Sentiment Index and the detected dominant cycle (208 days) via the Dynamic Cycle Explorer from WhenToTrade toolset

In theory, as with all sentiment vehicles, the scores work as contra-indicators. Thus, extreme points of bullishness should correspond to market tops, and extreme bearish composite scores should correspond to market bottoms. This is what we called the "hot-spots" of maximum financial risk or opportunity as shown in Chart 1 at the beginning of the article.

The window at the bottom of the chart shows the detected dominant cycle as a blue line. The indicator text shows that there is an underlying cycle with an active length of 208 days in the EUR/USD sentiment data set. The red plotted data behind the blue

89

cycle shows that we have a valid match between the ideal cycle and the real score movements on the sentiment. You can compare the highs and bottoms of this cycle match with major turns in the sentiment index. Thus, we have a clue to the fact that a 208-day cycle has driven social sentiment during the last three years. The most important point is the current day because we do not need a perfect fit in the distant past. Further, we know that cycles have a dynamic nature; therefore, the most important time period is the current past where the cycle parameters have to be in alignment with the real world.

Before we start to interpret the current conditions, though, we must check if this cycle – which is only related to social sentiment and has nothing to do with real price data – has correlations to turns in the price of EUR/USD currency pair.

Thus, Chart 4 shows the EUR/USD exchange rate plotted on top of this analysis.

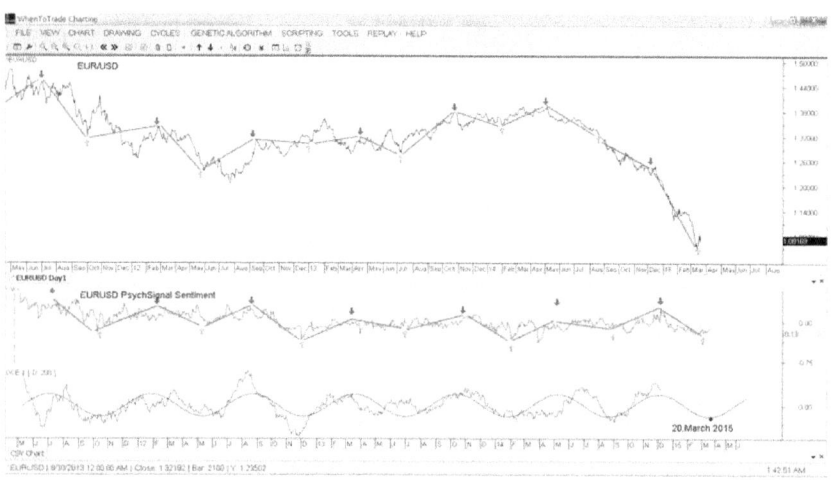

Chart 4: EUR/USD exchange rate turns in sync with detected sentiment cycle

The turns of the discovered dominant cycle are marked with red and green arrows on the price chart. We can see that we have an ideal fit between the social sentiment cycle and price turns of the currency pair. However, this cycle does not become visible on the exchange rate alone; further, the cycle does not predict the strength of each move. To see the situation more clearly, we have added a purple line to connect the arrows on the currency exchange rate.

In this context, it becomes clearly visible that it is more interesting to decipher the underlying pattern in the form of dynamic sentiment cycles than to try to interpret the raw sentiment data. In general, the raw turns of mood will not match price turns exactly because there are delays, noise, and distortions between mood and the unfolding events. Consequently, we are not interested in the micro turns of mood on the price chart; instead, we are looking for the general mood cycle to change its direction. These are what Dynamic Cycle Explorer is capable of detecting and tracking in real-time – a dynamic tool to detect cyclic points of maximum financial risk or opportunity.

It can be seen that we have a valid sentiment cycle of 208 days running – which points to the "hot-spot" of maximum financial opportunity at the day of the analysis.

As a result, we can pay close attention to where we are now in this sentiment cycle. The data analysis was done on March 20, 2015. The blue dot on the cycle marks the current day of the analysis.

The important point here is that the dominant cycle shows an imminent bottom with an extreme reading of bearishness. So we would expect the sentiment to rise over the next weeks with an expected price increase of EUR/USD happening in parallel. Thus, we would not expect the downtrend to resume shortly; instead, we would expect a major upswing in the currency pair that follows the dominant active sentiment pattern.

We now move forward two months and check the forecast. Chart 5 shows the same EUR/USD price that was shown at the beginning of this example and progresses it eight weeks to May 15, 2015.

Chart 5: EUR/USD price chart 8 weeks after forecast

The analysis has proved to be extremely accurate. The EUR/USD currency pair ended its long downtrend in March 2015 and started a strong upswing. Just six to eight weeks after the forecast, prices increased by more than +5%.

But not only did this analysis projected an upturn right on time. The cyclic sentiment analysis predicted the largest 30days price increase since 2013. (See chart 6)

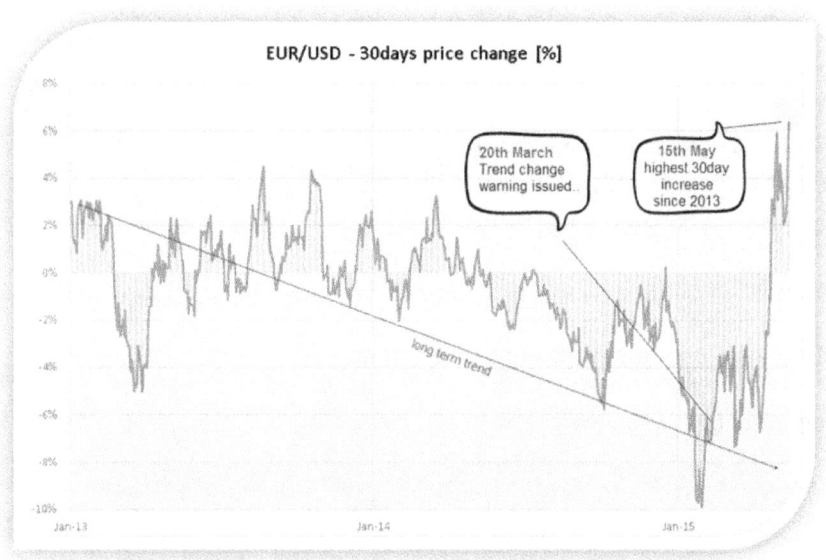

Chart 6: Biggest 30days gain in EUR/USD since 2013

It is important to mention that the cycle analysis shown in this article about EUR/USD sentiment was conducted live and in real time. This example was not cherry-picked. We alerted our community on Sunday, March 22 2015 before the market opened in the public open internet blog on PsychSignal, WhenToTrade and LinkedIn Pulse about this situation.

Therefore, this is a genuine and verifiable forecast based on the power of dynamic cycles and the new area of available sentiment data.

This article underpins the importance of cyclic research in social sentiment data sets in order to forecast important market turns. Thus, the combination of state-of-the-art sentiment data from PsychSignal with the latest cycle analysis and prediction tools from WTT delivers a truly unique view on financial markets.

If you are interested in learning more about dynamic cycles and the cycles detection algorithm used, we have published a book "Decoding The Hidden Market Rhythm – Part 1: Dynamic Cycles" on that topic available at Amazon here: http://amzn.com/1499283490.

Lars von Thienen

eMail: info@whentotrade.com

Website: https://www.whentotrade.com/

Chapter 11- Simple and Practical Tips to Easily and
Chapter 12 - Dramatically Improve Your Trading Psychology by Dr. Barry Burns

What Moves the Markets?

Do Fundamentals matter? Yes, but the information received is often late, can be revised, and may not even be accurate when released. It can also be hard to correlate with the movement of the market you're trading as we see that sometimes markets go up on bad news and down on good news!

So what really moves the markets if it's not a company's fundamentals or news?

Markets move on the actions people take based on their BELIEFS and FEELINGS about the market.

Of course being a massive auction house, no one person's actions move the market. The markets move as the result of LOTS of people – and therefore the markets move according to the principles of Mass Psychology.

This has led me to trade the markets using technical analysis rather than fundamental analysis.

Technical Analysis is the Math of Mass Psychology.

The "Nature" of the Markets

The movement of the market is the movement of mass psychology. So the "nature" of the market is HUMAN NATURE.

1. Charts are maps of collective human BEHAVIOR.

2. The market isn't LIKE people, it IS people.

3. Nothing gets plotted on a chart until people take ACTION.

4. Charts don't map people's thoughts, beliefs, hopes and fears ... they map COMMITMENTS!

The Nature of People

If the nature of the markets is the nature of people, it behooves us to ask about the nature of people. Here are five aspects of human nature and how those aspects are reflected in charts:

1. Goal Oriented – Trends

2. "3 Steps Forward, 2 Steps Back" – Oscillations

3. "Getting Stuck" – Consolidation

4. Work and Rest – Cycles

5. "All Nighters" and Vacation – Expanding and Contracting Cycles

6. Emotional Beings: Love and Hate, Overreact and passive aggressive – Market Bubbles

A Practical Exercise to Help You Think Different than the Masses:

It's no secret that most traders lose money. Trading is extremely risky and most people who attempt to make money in the markets end up losers. One of the keys to success, therefore, is to think different than the masses. You must be better than the "losers" (I don't use that term in a derogatory way, but simply in a literal way referring to those who consistently lose money).

Here's an exercise I engaged in for six months that helped me become familiar with how the losing traders are thinking and acting. I used this information to think and act differently than them. I invite you to do the same.

Attend several free live trading chat rooms where amateur traders are actively communicating with each other and watch the charts in conjunction with their comments.

Remember, the masses are wrong most of the time. So what you're hearing is the inner dialog and the behavior of the losers.

Do this for 3-6 months (listening to their comments and watching the charts in conjunction with their comments), and before long the sheer repetition of their same comments to the same price patterns will become engrained in your brain cells. You'll be able to hear their voices in your mind. Eventually you'll be able to do the reverse:

Without even being in the chat room, you'll be able to watch the charts, and in your mind hear the dialog of the losers!

The result is that you'll know what the losing traders are doing during certain price patterns (they're very consistent in doing the exact wrong things) and you can avoid making those mistakes yourself (and perhaps even take the opposite side of their trade).

In "Market Wizards," (Publisher: Wiley) Jack Schwager interviews some of the world's most successful traders in search of a commonality that can lead to success for others. His conclusion after the interviews:

"What set these traders apart? Most people think that winning in the markets has something to do with finding the secret formula. The truth is that any common denominator among the traders I interviewed had more to do with ATTITUDE than APPROACH."

In his follow-up book, "The New Market Wizards," (Publisher: HarperBusiness) Jack Schwager wrote:

"'We has met the enemy, and it is us.' The famous quote from Walt Kelly's cartoon strip, "Pogo," would provide as fitting a one-line summation of the art of trading as any. Time and time again, those whom I interviewed for this book and its predecessor stressed the absolutely critical role of psychological elements in trading success. When asked what was important to success, the Market Wizards never talked about indicators or techniques, but rather about such things as discipline, emotional control, patience, and mental attitude toward losing. The message is clear: The key to winning in the markets is internal, not external."

It's obvious that to be a successful trader, you need a viable trading method with setups, rules and a plan that works. Without that, no amount of "psychology" is going to help you.

Try Before You Buy

Unfortunately there are many traders who have a viable trading method, who never know it, because they have never tested the method divorced from their emotions.

For this reason I highly recommend paper trading any new method you're trying (even if you're a seasoned trader) for at least 3-6 months before you put a single real-money trade on the line. This paper trading must be done in real-time, not after the fact, so rather than literally using paper, I recommend you use a trading simulator or demo account to test drive your trading method.

This gives the additional benefit of helping you learn the timing of the entries. Learning to enter your orders without hesitation is a critical trading behavior for your success. It will also help you learn whether the methodology fits your personality.

By paper trading for 3-6 months, and keeping track of every trade (using trading logs), you'll find that the method works ... as long as you trade it without emotion.

Before you can trade successfully, you need to have confidence in your method. Without confidence in your method, you will second-guess the rules, get discouraged during draw downs, and fearfully stay out of good setups. The ONLY thing that will create that confidence is success. And the best way to achieve a winning track record is to trade without emotion ... and at the beginning, that means trading without money.

After successfully paper trading for an extended amount of time, it's time to start trading with a SMALL AMOUNT of real money. Now if you start losing, then you know the variable is the emotion of trading with money.

Once we solve the problem of finding a successful trading method, then we have to deal with the problem of YOU!

Overtrading is one of the biggest challenges to new traders. But one of the hallmarks of successful traders is that they actually trade very little. They wait for the PERFECT setups because they know that's the ONLY time that the odds are really with them, and that makes the difference between trading and gambling.

Even in the gambling world, however, the professionals know this. Profitable poker players fold on more hands than they play. If they don't have a strong opening hand with a high probability of winning, they simply fold and wait for a better one.

In his book, "Money Management for Gamblers (Publisher: Lyle Stuart), John Patrick writes:

"People who are way better educated than me rip my theories from here to Hades and back. They claim gambling is all math and statistical analysis. They will never grasp the true meaning of gambling – because they have never been there.

... People who think that a math equation is gonna give them a leg up on winning ought have that leg whack them in the area where they sit on their brains.

... you absolutely must have money management ... Topped off with a healthy dose of discipline."

... [The pros] don't make MISTAKES, and they don't have tells. Patience is a virtue, stupidity is a one-way street to disaster, talk is minimal, and mercy is absent. Make a MISTAKE and seven vultures circle the wagons, waiting to divide the spoils. When the night is done and you are fortunate enough to escape with a small profit, the ride home gives you only a short time to count your blessings and your money."

If you're trading every day of the week and you're not trading well with a successful methodology, it's most likely because you're making mistakes.

So is there a way to eliminate mistakes? No one ever becomes a perfect trader, but the first step to reducing your mistakes is to identify them.

Here are10 Commandments which are general rules. We'll translate them into specific "mistakes" as they would relate to the rules of our trading methodology.

1. Don't Chase a Move.

2. Don't Trade Choppy Markets.

3. Don't Fight the Trend.

4. Don't Trade Too Many Contracts for Your Account Size.

5. Don't Trade for the "Action."

6. Do Guard Your Capital; it's Your Lifeblood.

7. Don't Try to Recover Losses with Emotional "Revenge Trading."

8. Don't Trade the Market, Only Trade Your Rules.

9. Don't Place Your Stops Too Close.

10. Don't Take Profits Too Soon.

One of my favorite sayings in trading is:

"Successful Trading is Simply a Matter of NOT MAKING MISTAKES."

I have found this to be a great truism in my trading life. As long as I don't make mistakes, I come out ahead at the end of the week or month. Of course that is predicated on the issue of first having a viable trading methodology.

The "mistakes" I refer to are the 10 Commandments listed above. This is my list which reflects the most common mistakes I found myself making. I compiled this list from other traders and my own experience. I encourage you to add or subtract to it. Make it your own. Use this as a springboard for creating your own list that aligns with your own unique trading struggles.

Your goal is to trade your method as strictly as possible and without making any of these mistakes.

Avoiding mistakes is a matter of self-discipline.

Although I can't give you self-discipline, I will give you an exercise that can help you tremendously with the issue. You still have to actually stick to it, but if nothing else it can serve as a mirror to reflect back to you how out of control your trading may actually be.

The exercise is simple. Keep a trading log of every trade you take. Rather than simply recording your entry and exit prices and times, also record any mistakes you made on each trade (refer to the "10 Commandments" above for a list of mistakes). \

At the end of each day, transfer the results of your trading day, including your mistakes, to a weekly trading log where you record the summary of your trading day on one row.

Over time, you'll notice patterns of mistakes you make consistently that you're not currently consciously aware of.

Finally, subtract all the losses of trades in which you made mistakes, and see what you're trading income would be without those trades. In many cases, people find that they'd be successful traders right now if they simply eliminated their mistakes!

Here are sample copies of my trading logs. You're welcome to use these or create your own:

DAILY TRADING LOG

DATE: _____/_____/_____

Successful Trading is Simply a Business of NOT MAKING MISTAKES
That's what separates the pro who makes money from the educated amateur.

TIMES OF ECONOMIC REPORTS:

1. _____ 3. _____
2. _____ 4. _____

ENTRY TIME	TRADING VEHICLE	LONG/SHORT ENTRY PRICE	PROTECTIVE STOP	1ST TARGET	2ND TARGET	EXIT TIME	EXIT PRICE	$ GAIN/LOSS	TOTAL GAIN/LOSS

NOTES: | MISTAKES:

ENTRY TIME	TRADING VEHICLE	LONG/SHORT ENTRY PRICE	PROTECTIVE STOP	1ST TARGET	2ND TARGET	EXIT TIME	EXIT PRICE	$ GAIN/LOSS	TOTAL GAIN/LOSS

NOTES: | MISTAKES

ENTRY TIME	TRADING VEHICLE	LONG/SHORT ENTRY PRICE	PROTECTIVE STOP	1ST TARGET	2ND TARGET	EXIT TIME	EXIT PRICE	$ GAIN/LOSS	TOTAL GAIN/LOSS

NOTES: | MISTAKES

TRADE LOG FOR THE WEEK OF _____ to _____

DATE	WIN/LOSS	TOTAL P/L	AVERAGE $ WIN/$LOSS	COM-MISS	NET P/L: % ACCT	# OF MIS-TAKES	NET P/L w/o MIS-TAKES	MISTAKES
WEEK TOTALS								

Dr. Barry Burns is the owner of Top Dog Trading, the author of "Trend Trading for Dummies," has presented seminars for the Chicago Mercantile Exchange, the Eurex Exchange, MetaStock and trading expos around the country.

CHAPTER 13 - SONATA TRADING COMPUTER BY LARRY JACOBS

Traders World now has the new powerful Sonata Trading Computer Silent workstation series perfect for traders. Let me explain why you need one.

The Sonata is focused on high performance, reliability and value which are the requirements of our demanding traders.

Traders World is celebrating its 29th year of operation. The first computers we sold for trading were the Apple IIe when they first came out. Through the years we have perfected the trading computer to what it is today.

These new workstations achieve 3 goals:

1. These are powerful user-friendly dream systems, featuring Intel's fastest CPUs. They come in both 4-core and 6-core models which are full featured yet very affordable professional trading computers and they support up to 8 monitors.

2. They have top reliability featuring rock solid fully integrated Asus motherboards. Asus is now considered the best motherboard available. They are more reliable, faster and last much longer than any other ones. Asus enables Traders World to ship the finest workstations with Intel i7 CPUs in tandem with the fastest solid state drives by Samsung. The Sonata also integrates the latest liquid CPU cooling with advanced cooling to achieve a

nearly silent operation. No other trading computer is as quiet and as powerful as the Sonata.

3. These Sonata Trading Computers are a great value and you can get 100% money back through TradeStation rebates. Traders can apply their full purchase of the Sonata including monitor screens toward TradeStation commissions, making these powerful computers essentially free over time for active traders. Also traders can purchase the systems through PayPal and get 6 months of free interest.

As an industry leader for multiple monitor trading computers, Traders World is delighted to provide our traders with the fastest performance that they need to be successful in these fast moving markets where micro seconds can make winners from losers. The Sonata Trading Computer exploits every known technology to help traders analyze the markets in real time, enabling much quicker decisions, much faster algorithmic trading and increased speed of order execution. A significant amount of research is constantly done to make sure the Sonata has the latest and best technology.

As you probably know today's volatile markets are dominated by high-frequency trading. Success is determined by both timing and quick decisions. Once traders determine their strategies and methods for trading, the speed of execution using high end trading computers is essential and the Sonata is the king here.

Our goal was to deliver the world's fastest and most reliable trading workstation at the best price. Our prices are the exceptionally low in the industry even though the parts we use are higher quality than most competitors. Our challenge is to deliver the best for the least. Clearly the Sonata is the best trading workstation available we have ever delivered for the price. Going even further I think the Sonata is the best workstation bar non for the trader. It really crushes any alternative trading computer today from competitors.

The Sonata can drive up to 8 independent monitors and can be bundled in complete packages with our stands.

Now let me explain what goes into the Sonata Trading Computer and why.

First the case is very important. We use the best case available the Fractal Design R4 Black Pearl. The case is nearly silent because the side and front panels are fitted with dense, sound-absorbing material making it a benchmark for noise reduction. Multiple-ventilation keeps the components safe at optimal temperatures. The case is made with precision components from Sweden. No other case compares for the trader. Silence is golden.

Next we use the best motherboards from Asus. My favorite is the
Sabertooth X99-A. It has a TUF Engine Power Design with the
Ultimate Cool Thermal Solution. It supports the 4th generation
Intel i7 CPUs and 32GB of DDR3 memory. It is made of military
strong components, better than any other motherboard made
today.

As for memory we use the best Corsair Vengeance DDR3 SDRAM 1866 MHz memory. It is super-fast and reliable.

The processor we use is the Intel Core i7-4770K Haswell 3.5GHz processor. It gives you the trader maximized performance and the ability to run multiple demanding tasks with ease. It uses Intel's Hyper-Threading Technology to power the PC to keep pace with any trading demand without slowing down. It gives you the power to trade and can be easily overclocked to 4.5GHz.

The Sonata has the best Solid State Drives, the Samsung Pro 840 Series. The technology used is above any of the competition. It gives the Sonata performance that no one ever thought possible. This SSD enables the computer to boot up amazingly in as little as 15 seconds and run trading programs as fast as possible. This allows the computer to display charts and data with virtually no delay and gives traders very fast execution.

The Sonata uses Asus 750TI Powerful Graphics many times more powerful than the graphics used by others for multiple monitors. The Sonata can hold two of these giving the maximum output to 8 monitors.

The Sonata uses the best Air cooled CPU Cooler on the Market.

The Sonata is powered by the Corsair CS Series Power Supply. It is 85% energy and is efficient for low noise and power bills. It provides clean and reliable power.

The Sonata used the Asus VN247-P 23.6-inch screens with a super narrow frame. Best for use in multiple monitor trading with full

1080p visual quality. Has ultra-fast 1ms response time for amazingly blur-free trading experience.

Check out what our customers say see testimonials:

http://sonatatradingcomputers.com/TESTIMONIALS.html

Why settle for anything less than a Sonata Trading Computer.

For more information go to
http://www.SonataTradingComputers.com

Chapter 14 - Anatomy of a Trading Loss by Adrienne Toghraie

In every performance based endeavor there is the chance that loss will occur. This is certainly true for those who are traders. In trading, it is more accurate to say when loss occurs, not that there is a chance that loss will occur. While a loss can feel devastating when it occurs, what you do after will determine whether you let the loss defeat you, or you treat it as part of the overall win towards your desired goal.

Let's look at several scenarios that a trader can experience when a loss occurs.

First phase

• A well-defined and tested strategy before a loss occurs

• See an opportunity based on a strategy

• Know the monetary risk involved for this particular trade

• Feel good about the prospects of the outcome of the trade

• Take the trade with a pre-determined stop in place

• Stopped out with a loss

A loss that occurs because the rules of a strategy have been violated, or there is no predetermined tested strategy:

- Get into a trade on a whim

- Get in too late

- Miscalculate the risk when getting into a trade

- Get out too early

- Clerical error

- Have no stops, change the stop

Second phase

- You have taken the loss and now you (On the positive side):

- Look for the next opportunity

- Take a predetermined break that you have established in your business plan for when you take a loss, and then begin looking for the next opportunity

You have taken the loss and now you (On the negative side):

- Get mentally and sometimes physically upset looping a story in your mind about the loss

- Take responsibility for the loss and condemn yourself

- Blame someone else and direct all your bad feelings towards him or her

Third phase

- Handling the mental aspect (On the positive side)

• Know that losses are a part of the overall win and look for another opportunity

• Learn a lesson that you will not repeat and keep trading

• Realize that you must have a tested strategy and stop trading to put together a plan

Handling the mental aspect (On the negative side):

• Go to a dark place inside of yourself where you have placed losses of the past, and then get emotionally upset out of proportion

• Stay in a loop of upset, and then try to get back at the markets

• Continue trading in ignorance creating more losses

• Stop trading altogether

Facing losses from the beginning

Sandra knew from the start that losses would be the largest hurdle that she would face in becoming a trader. She made it a priority to speak to other traders about it and worked with a coach before she took her first trade. As part of her trading business plan she created every scenario for contingencies in dealing with loss.

Sandra's father, who was an avid baseball fan, kept reminding her that seventy percent of the best baseball players lose and still have great performance records. With her father's encouragement and her own due diligence, Sandra started her trading career with the best preparation for taking losses.

Conclusion

Losses are a part of what a trader must face in order to become successful. How a trader handles those losses will determine how long it takes him to get there.

Adrienne's Free Webinars

Adrienne presents free webinars on the psychology of trading

Email Adrienne@TradingOnTarget.com

CHAPTER 15 – ACTIVITY BASED TRADING SUCCESS BY THOMAS BARMANN

As a trader or investor, you are constantly predicting the future outcome of today's asset price situations.

You basically have two potential ways of estimating the future price move of an asset:

Way-1: Fundamental Analysis

Way-2: Technical Analysis

In our presentation and article, we focus purely on technical analysis and lead you to a new way of viewing and predicting: Activity Based Trading.

Alternating asset prices are based on changes in supply and demand patterns:

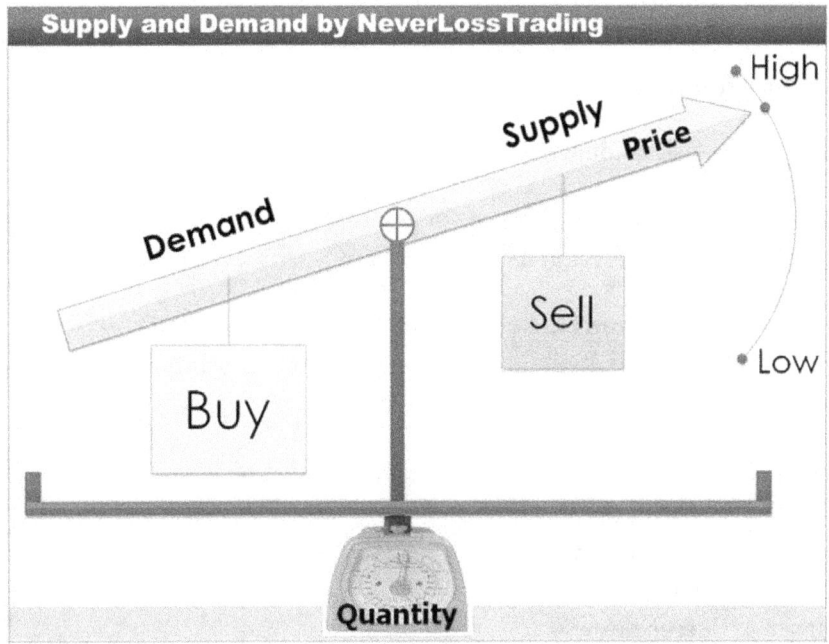

The key to successful trading is finding assets, which have a change in their supply and demand pattern that is resulting in a price change.

How to get there?

By using algorithmic based computer programs that focus on finding those assets and highlight potential entry- and exit points; pairing this information with a sound knowledge of the behavior pattern of key market participants: A trading system.

To establish a constant income from trading, your system shall provide you with:

First: Defined entries/exits/stops

Second: Probabilities of trade setups

Third: Clear risk guidance rules for preventing draw downs

To understand behavior patterns of key market participants, let us make a short excursion into base economic rules:

Pareto Principle: In an efficient economic situation like the Financial Markets, individuals are maximizing their utility. The final 85% of all market transactions are executed by institutional investors. This accounts for all markets:

Market-1: Stocks
Market-2: Commodities
Market-3: Treasuries
Market-4: Currencies

Let us take an overview of the world's biggest financial institutions:

Worlds biggest Institutional Investors

Institution	Sector Focus	Country
Goldman Sachs	Investments, Funds	USA
JP Morgan Chase Manhattan	Banking, Investments, Funds	USA
Bank of America	Banking, Investments	USA
Merrill Lynch	Investments, Funds	USA
Deutsche Bank	Banking, Investments	Germany
UBS AG	Banking, Investments	Switzerland
Barclays Capital	Banking, Investmetns, Funds	UK
Royal Bank of Scotland	Banking, Investments, Funds	Scotland
Citi	Banking, investments	USA
Pimco	Funds	USA
Fidelity	Funds	USA
Vanguard	Funds	USA
Spider	Funs	USA
Bridgwarter Assiciates	Funds	USA
BNP Paribas	Banking, Investments	France

* Funds: Hedge Funds, Mutual Funds, Exchange Traded Funds

The market action and role of the listed institutions varies and we differentiate:

Leaders, who are the key decision makers and initiate change.

Gatekeepers, who facilitate and partially control the action.

Followers, who spot and follow key market action.

Based on their specific role and market action, we can differentiate the following categories:

Institutional Investors by Category

Category	Characteristic	Examples (Stock Symbol)	Institutional Focus
Prop Traders	Leading institutions , trading "their own money"	GS, MS, DB, UBS, CS	Finding best performers: Stocks or Industry Sectors
Fund Managers	Pension Funds, Mutual Funds, ETF's, Hedge Funds	OPY, ING, SPY, BLK	Following Indexes: S&P 500, Small Caps, Countries
Low Risk Investors	Insurances, Banks	AIG, ALV.DE, UNH, PRU, BAC, WFC, C	Capital investment with low risk tolerance.
Liquidity Providers	Market Makers, ECN's, Wholesalers	JPM, UBS, CME,BCS	Offering at the bid and ask. Again, we find "Prop Trading" companies.

By the sheer size of transactions institutions need to go through when making a shift in an asset: buying or selling; their action leaves an activity based pattern on the chart, which you can learn to spot and follow.

When institutional activity can be displayed on your chart, it can be taken as base for your trading or investing decisions.

This is why we are not leaning towards using fundamental analysis. Institutions are in a much better position to equate and decide on fundamental analysis then private investors can do. When their action is displayed on the chart, we can just go and follow.

At times people ask us: Where is your competitive advantage, when you are following institutional investments?

The answer is:

As a private investor, we hold much smaller positions and can transact entire investments at once; entering and exiting much faster and on an average better price base than institutional investors can.

The odds are in your favor: Make use of this knowledge.

The NLT Activity Based Trading System helps you to identify key price turning points with specific entries, exits, stops, on high probability setups.

Here are some examples of how institutional action can be displayed and followed from your chart;

Goldman Sachs, Traded from the 1-Hour Chart

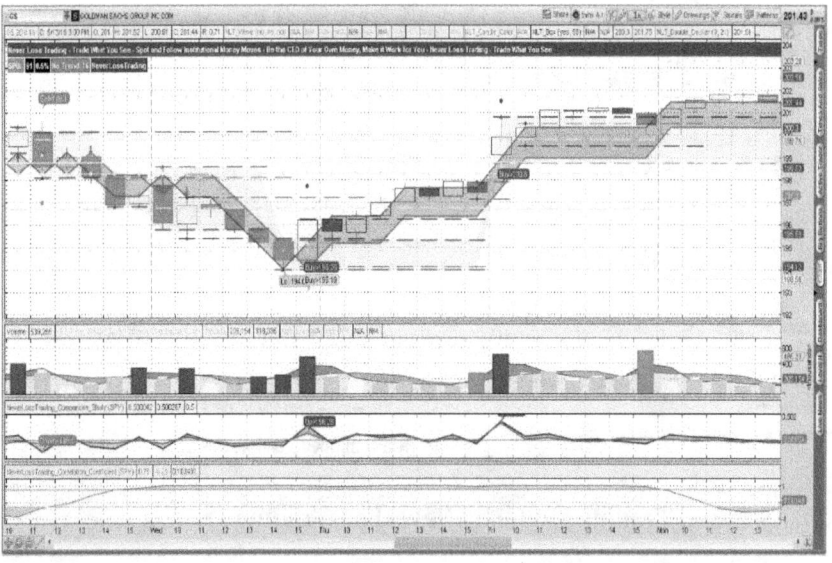

The chart shows three trade entry points from the left to the right and we only trade when this price threshold is surpassed in the candle following the trade initiation candle:

Sell < 198.10. Lead to a trade.

Buy > 196.26. Lead to a trade.

Buy > 200.80. No trade.

Why do we only trade if the spelled out price threshold is surpassed?

We want confirmation that the new direction initiated is followed by key market participants, applying the following principles:

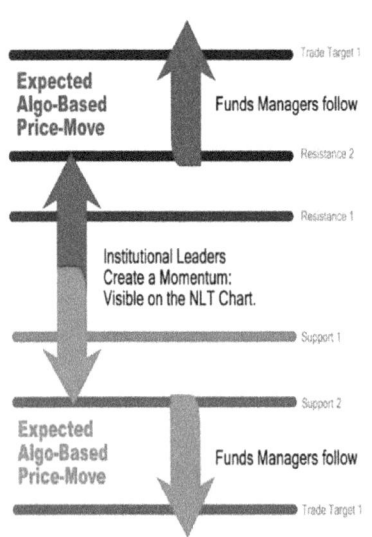

1. **Prices accumulate** prior to a price move and our indicators are identifying this stage by measuring price-, volume- and volatility development, with the NLT-specific market pressure model.

2. Prices **test** the **high/low** of a range prior to breakout. Again, our sensors are triggered and alarm us.

3. Breakout to the next price increment. It shows and is highlighted right on our charts and picked up by our scanners.

4. The **price breakout is noticed** by key market participants and is either:
   - Confirmed **– and we trade it.**
   - **Not confirmed** – and we stay out.

Activity Based Trading Model by NeverLossTrading

Aside from the price threshold for the trade entry, our system as all trading systems shall do, provides clearly defined exits and stop-levels:

NLT Swing Trading Chart with Red Stop Lines

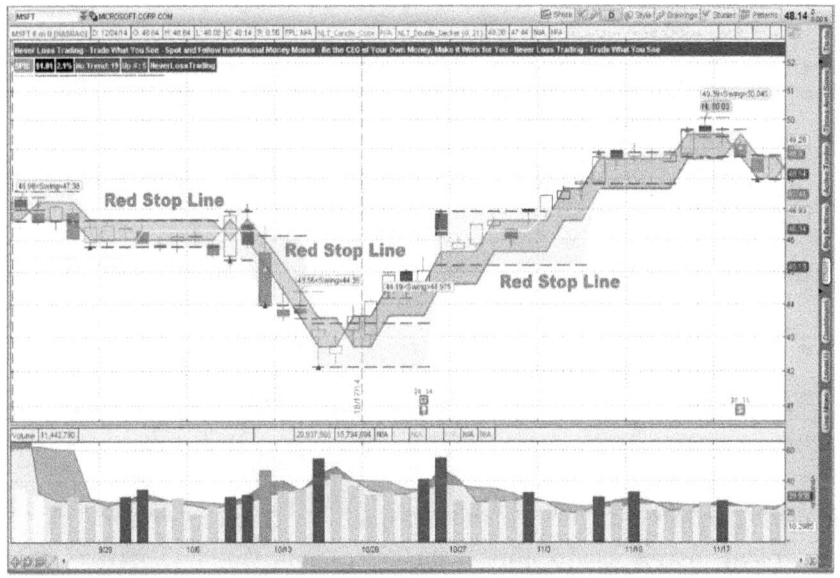

Positive exits for trades are put on the chart by either a highlighted dot or they are represented by a gray NLT Box Line.

NLT Activity Based Trading Chart with Entries and Exits

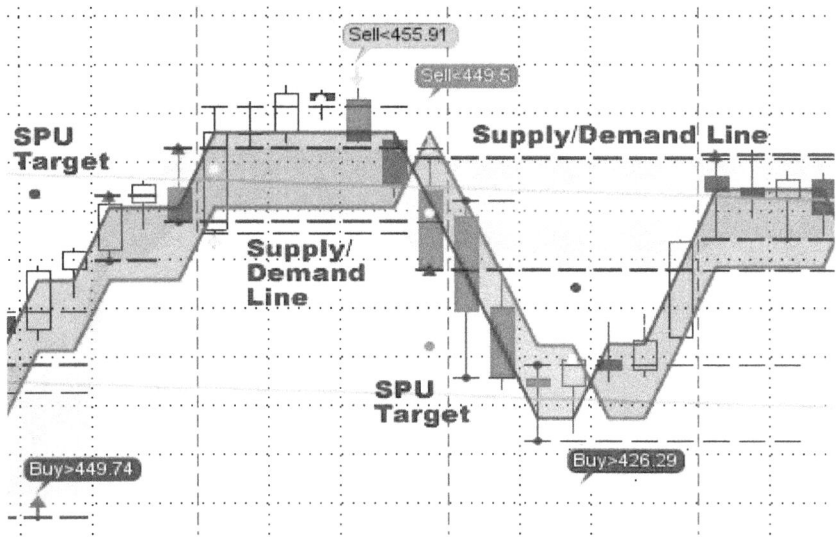

Repetitive action with focus on high probability trade setups on defined entries, exits, and stops is the key to your trading success.

The big advantage of an Activity Based Trading System: Institutions make a price move, you spot it and you follow: Fast entry and exit.

When you are using a mathematical based trading system, you compare the price development with a constant correlation over a period of time until you recognize price changes, which is usual resulting in late entries and exits.

Take a look on a side by side comparison, where we painted a moving averaged based system aside from a pattern based system: Both try to force feed a pre-defined behavior and trade pattern, while the activity based trading system, spots and follows market action instantaneously.

Trading Systems Compared

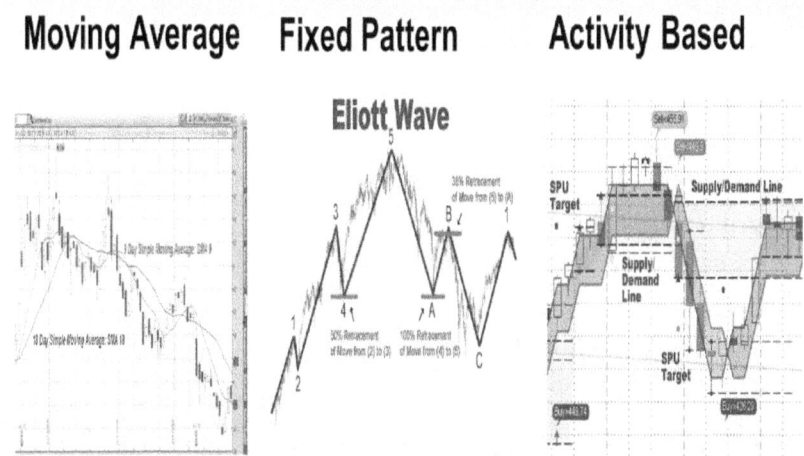

Moving Average   **Fixed Pattern**   **Activity Based**

Markets can follow a pattern, but they don't have to. High probability trading is reached by focusing on the market action of now and translating this into evaluating and trading opportunities that arise.

After using the right trading system, your key actions to trading success are:

• Be a Probability Thinker
• Act as your own Analyst (short-, long-term)
• Stay Engaged (constant investment)
• Know and Apply Trade Adjustment Methods

A) Be a Probability Thinker

Probability = Measure of the likeliness that an event will occur.

At a probability to win > 50%, participation rate is key.

Participation Rate: Number of opportunities you can compete for per time unit observed.

How to determine the probability of a trade setup?

• Back test 100 trades
• Forward test 10 trades
• Strike a balance: Winners vs. Losers (%)
• Golden Rule:
• Probability of the Trade Setup (past performance) x Reward / (Risk x Probability of Failing) > 1.5

Then bring the probability for success in relation with the reward and risk of a trade, you can decide for your position size, always considering that capital preservation is key. See the stop line example in the above chart.

When you come to using a high probability trading system your odds of winning should be at least two out of three trades. To bring your trade to target, you need to give the price move an adequate wiggle room; however, when you never risk more than 1.2-times your reward, you are paving the way to success:

Calculation Example: 100 Trades
Reward: $1 x 0.67 x 100 = $67
Risk (max) $1.2 x 0.33 x 100 = $40
Expected Result: $27

Isn't that a clear way of focusing on making money? In our mentorship classes, we develop specific asset based and investment based business plans with you, which help you to focus and allocate your time to trading.

B) Acting as Being Your Own Analyst

You are the captain of your trades and investments: Never leave the final decisions up to a computer:

Computers are great to run and extract opportunities; however, they are lacking eyes to oversee and relate to the general market environment in recognizing key supply and demand levels; hence, it is you who makes the final decision:

Computers are faster, humans are smarter.

You want to trade what you see and learn how to know in advance where price accumulation will most likely take place; how to take advantage of this knowledge by exiting profitable trades right there instead of initiating trades where you have a high probability of a potential reversal move, triggered by institutional orders.

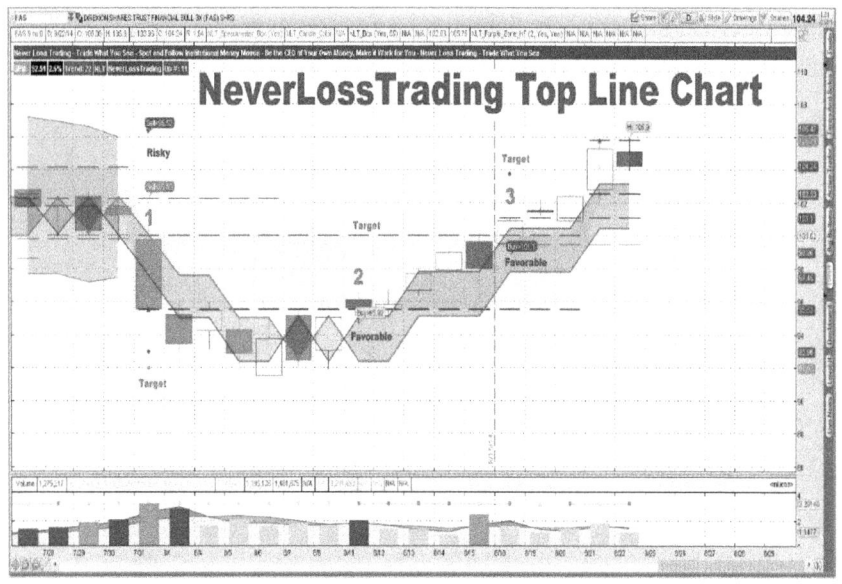

NeverLossTrading Top-Line Chart with Trade Initiation Signals
and Trade Targets

From the left to the right, you see:

Sell 95.52: A risky setup where the stop leads to an unfavorable
reward/risk scenario. The trade still worked and concluded at the
set target: red dot.

Buy 95.92: A favorable setup with much higher reward than risk.
A positive trade.

Buy 101.10: An acceptable setup with a balanced reward to risk.
Another winner.

Targets are specifically marked by the NLT Software.

Seeing this, I hope you agree: It is more easy to trade what you see!

C) Stay Engaged

Finding trading opportunities is a key challenge for every trader or investor. You are facing a wide variety of choices:

40,000 US-Stocks

3,500 ETF's

200 Futures

78 FOREX Pairs

Basically, you need to use a fish finder, giving you assets ready to evaluate for trading based on your trading system setup.

At NeverLossTrading we support you threefold:

One: Daily NLT Alerts are notifying you about assets that show the specific chart conditions you are looking for.

Two: You scan for assets with institutional attention, using the scanners that are built in the NLT Top-Line system.

Three: We work out a specific portfolio of assets with you and you check the charts on the reference time frame.

Speaking for myself, I am investing about two hour per day, six days a week for finding assets ready to trade. If you subscribe to one of our NLT Alert services, reaching from $99 to $ 495, the associated costs are $2 to $10 per hour.

As a special offer to you: If you are interested in receiving one the NLT Alerts free for one week, write and email specifying the NLT Alert you want to receive: contact@NeverLossTrading.com and check your inbox.

NLT Alerts spell out the specific chart conditions they derive from and propose price thresholds for entry and stop, calculating reward/risk and return opportunity. They are Excel based, allowing you to filter and sort:

Primary Signal Symbols	Secondary Signal Symbols	Sentiment	Trade Setup	Option Trading Conditions	NASDAQ Stock	P/E Ratio	P/C Ratio	Evaluation	NLT Box Trend	Relation to History	Sector	Primary NLT Signal	Secondary NLT Signal	Last	Daily SPU	Daily SPU to Last %	Move to Last %	Approx. 1 Hour SPU	1-Hour SPU to Last	Trade Direction	NLT Momentum	NLT Trend	Strongest NLT Indicator	NLT Purple Zone	NLT Volatility	NLT Volume Indicator
BHP		Bull	Strong	Excellent	10		1.09	Mid-Range	Down	Above (st)	Metals &	Power		$ 50.27	$ 1.22	2.4%	93.4%	$ 0.46	0.9%	Up	down	up	Power		Breakout	>Average
	CMG	Bull	Strong	Potential	41		1.09	Bottom R	Down	Way Below	Hotels,		Early up	$ 628.82	$ 13.88	2.2%	11.5%	$ 5.27	0.8%	Up	down	Early up	Early up			Diff. Up
LEN		Bull	Favorable	Potential	16		0.24	Bottom R	Down	Below	Household	Power		$ 46.47	$ 1.17	2.5%	100.9%	$ 0.44	1.0%	Up	HF up	down	Power		Strong Up	
	DHI	Bull	Favorable	Potential	16		0.66	Bottom R	Down	Way Below	Household		Early up	$ 25.72	$ 0.75	2.9%	60.0%	$ 0.29	1.1%	Up	new up	Early up	Early up			
UNPR		Bull	Favorable		(35)		1.58	Bullish Cu	Up	Above (S)	Commun		Diff. Up	$ 26.73	$ 0.63	2.4%	9.2%	$ 0.25	0.9%	Up	new up	up	Diff. Up		Strong Up	Diff. Up
BBY		Bull	Acceptable		10		0.79	Bottom R	Down	Below	Specialty	Power		$ 36.12	$ 0.75	2.1%	106.7%	$ 0.29	0.8%	Up	HF up	down	Power		Strong Up	
	TEVA	Bear	Acceptable	Potential	0		0.77	Weakness	Down	Below	Pharmac	Diff.		$ 60.04	$ 1.71	2.8%	6.4%	$ 0.65	1.1%	Down	down	down	Diff.			Diff. Down
	HES	Bear	Acceptable	Acceptable	23		0.93	Weakness	Down	Cutting Be	Oil, Gas	End		$ 73.46	$ 1.97	2.7%	51.3%	$ 0.75	1.0%	Down	down	down	End	EndChan	Strong Dow	Diff. Down
	FCX	Bear	Acceptable	Excellent	(6)		0.52	Top Weak	Up	Above	Metals &		Early	$ 22.91	$ 0.85	3.7%	41.2%	$ 0.32	1.4%	Down	new	Early	Early			
MA		Bull	Acceptable	Acceptable	28		1.09	Bullish Cu	Up	Cutting A	IT	HF up		$ 92.05	$ 1.76	1.9%	84.1%	$ 0.67	0.7%	Up	HF up	up	HF up		Strong Up	
	MDT	Bull	Acceptable	Acceptable	34		0.96	Bottom R	Up	Cutting A	Health	Diff. Up		$ 74.60	$ 1.36	1.8%	20.6%	$ 0.52	0.7%	Up	down	down	Diff. Up		Strong Up	Diff. Up
COF		Bear	Acceptable	Potential	11		0.75	Top Weak	Up	Below	Consume		HF down	$ 82.02	$ 1.09	1.3%	20.2%	$ 0.41	0.5%	Down	HF down	HF down			Strong Dow	>Average
LIEN		Bull	Acceptable		(60)		0.23	Bullish Cu	Up	Above	Commun	HF up		$ 21.43	$ 0.38	2.7%	58.6%	$ 0.22	1.0%		HF up	new up	HF up		Strong Up	

Primary Signal Symbols	Secondary Signal Symbols	Volume (mill.)	Actual Move	Last Price	Critical Price Point	Chritical Price Move	Entry Price	Target Price-1	Price Move to Target	Return at Target-1	Stop Approx.	% Risk at 1-SPU	Reward to Risk	Odds Evaluation	Last Hours Price Move	Last-4 Hours Price Move	Option Feedback	Exp. Option Price > 30 Days	Exp. Option Price ^20 Days	Exp. Option Price < 14 Days	Weekly Options	Comment	
BHP		1.4	-2.2%	$ 50.27	$ 50.32	$ 0.07	$ 50.34	$ 51.49	$ 1.15	2.3%	$ 49.55	1.6%	1.0:6	Strong			good valu	$ 1.42	$ 1.02	0.85		Reached Target	Win
	CMG	2.9	0.3%	$ 628.82	$ 633.41	$ 4.87	$ 633.69	$ 647.29	$ 13.60	2.1%	$ 625.39	1.3%	1.0:6	Strong			good valu	$ 16.19	$ 11.57	9.72	Yes	Reached Target	Win
LEN		5.9	2.6%	$ 46.47	$ 46.62	$ 0.17	$ 46.64	$ 47.64	$ 1.00	2.1%	$ 45.21	3.1%	1:1.4	Favorable			good valu	$ 1.37	$ 0.98	0.82	Yes	Gapped up too far	No Trade
	DHI	2.6	1.8%	$ 25.72	$ 25.81	$ 0.11	$ 25.83	$ 26.56	$ 0.73	2.8%	$ 25.19	2.5%	1:0.8	Favorable			good valu	$ 0.88	$ 0.63	0.53	Yes	Small Gap	Win
	UNPR	0	0.2%	$ 26.73	$ 26.89	$ 0.17	$ 26.90	$ 27.22	$ 0.31	1.2%	$ 26.66	0.9%	1:0.7	Favorable			good valu	$ 0.76	$ 0.54	0.46	Yes	Reached Target	Win
BBY		18.2	2.3%	$ 36.12	$ 36.23	$ 0.13	$ 36.25	$ 36.87	$ 0.63	1.7%	$ 35.21	2.9%	1.1:6	Acceptable		BBY	good valu	$ 0.88	$ 0.63	0.53	Yes	Reached Target	Win
	TEVA	0	-0.2%	$ 60.04	$ 59.76	$ (0.31)	$ 59.73	$ 58.91	$ 0.82	1.4%	$ 60.57	1.4%	1:1	Acceptable		TEVA	good valu	$ 2.00	$ 1.43	1.20	Yes	Stopped	Loss
	HES	0	-1.4%	$ 73.46	$ 72.74	$ (0.76)	$ 72.70	$ 70.77	$ 1.93	2.7%	$ 74.67	2.7%	1:1	Acceptable			good valu	$ 2.30	$ 1.64	1.38	Yes	Reached Target	Win
	FCX	3	-1.5%	$ 22.91	$ 22.48	$ (0.45)	$ 22.46	$ 21.63	$ 0.83	3.7%	$ 23.31	3.8%	1:1	Acceptable			good valu	$ 0.99	$ 0.71	0.60	Yes	Not Confirmed	No Trade
MA		4.1	1.8%	$ 92.05	$ 92.16	$ 0.15	$ 92.20	$ 93.92	$ 1.72	1.9%	$ 90.35	2.0%	1:1	Acceptable			good valu	$ 2.05	$ 1.47	1.23	Yes	Gapped up	Win
	MDT	0	0.4%	$ 74.60	$ 74.81	$ 0.24	$ 74.84	$ 75.49	$ 0.65	0.9%	$ 74.09	1.0%	1:1.1	Acceptable		MDT	good valu	$ 1.59	$ 1.13	0.95	Yes	Gapped up	Win
COF		2.9	-0.3%	$ 82.02	$ 81.40	$ (0.64)	$ 81.38	$ 80.31	$ 1.07	1.3%	$ 82.47	1.3%	1:1	Acceptable			good valu	$ 1.27	$ 0.91	0.76	Yes	Opposite Move	No Trade
LIEN		5.5	1.6%	$ 21.43	$ 21.51	$ 0.09	$ 21.52	$ 22.09	$ 0.57	2.6%	$ 20.92	2.8%	1:1	Acceptable			good valu	$ 0.68	$ 0.48	0.41		Gapped up	Win

Example: NLT Alert for May 8, 2015, issued on May 7 at 7 p.m. EST; 9 wins, 1 loss

The last column of the lower table shows if the trade price threshold was surpassed and thus a chance for a trade was giving with its outcome in relation to the originally set target.

The above report is called NLT Stock Alert and highlights stocks with favorable setups according to the NLT Top-Line and HF System. Aside from subscribing to this alerts as a NeverLossTrading user, you make use of them by the spelled out price threshold and target, even so you are not having the NLT chart view available. If you like to take advantage of a free week of our service, please write us an email, specifying the NLT Alert you prefer to receive:

contact@NeverLossTrading.com

D) Know and Apply Trade Adjustment Methods

Teaching people how to adjust a trade instead of taking a loss when the trade goes against you is the basis of our name: NeverLossTrading.

A) Stock Trades can be adjusted without the need for additional capital.

B) Option Trades can be adjusted with minimum Margin requirements.

C) On Futures Trades only specific assets can be adjusted, the majority cannot be adjusted, you exit at the stop.

Imagine how trading will be for you, if you know and apply methods to:

Adjustment-1: Reduce the Risk to Half
Adjustment-2: Reduce the Risk to Zero
Adjustment-3: Turn Losers into Winners

To demonstrate what applying trade adjustments to your bad trades can do for you let us give a couple of calculation examples:

Example-1: Stock Trading Adjustment

Base-1: Average Risk and Reward for a stock trade from a daily chart: 2%

Base-2: Assumed Probability for success: 67%

Base-3: Calculation on 100 Trades

Calculation-1; No Adjust: (100 x 0.67 x 2%) – (100 x 0.33 x 2%) = 68%

Calculation-2; 50% Loss: (100 x 0.67 x 2%) – (100 x 0.33 x 1%) = 101%

Calculation-3; No Loss: (100 x 0.67 x 2%) – (100 x 0.33 x 0%) = 134%

The stock trading example shows that applying trade adjustment methods better your expected returns by 50% – 110%, giving your trading a total different outlook.

When we measure the impact of applying trade adjustment methods on option-trades, it is even more drastic. See the following example:

Example-1: Stock Trading Adjustment
Base-1: Average Reward: 35%
Base-2: Average Risk: 60%
Base-3: High Probability Setup: >67%
Base-4: Calculation on 100 Trades:

Calculation-1; No Adjust: $(100 \times 0.67 \times 35\%) - (100 \times 0.33 \times 60\%)$ = 365%

Calculation-2; 50% Loss: $(100 \times 0.67 \times 35\%) - (100 \times 0.33 \times 30\%)$ = 1355%

Calcualtion-2; No Loss: $(100 \times 0.67 \times 35\%) - (100 \times 0.33 \times 0\%)$ = 2345%

Those numbers just speak for themselves, telling you to no more trade options without knowing from the get go where you adjust a trade in case the price move of the underlying goes against you.

Unfortunately many new option traders use neither a high probability system nor know how to apply adjustment methods. If this is the case, you might not wonder why option trading can have a quick negative impact on you:

Option trading with 55% probability for success, not applying trade adjustments:

No Adjust: $(100 \times 0.55 \times 35\%) - (100 \times 0.45 \times 60\%) = -775\%$

Hence, there is no way of winning long-term.

The specific action steps to applying trade adjustments are taught in the NeverLossTrading mentorships.

Summary:

To trade with the odds in your favor:

Action-1: Use and apply our Activity Based Trading System: which helps you to spot and follow institutional actions.

Action-2: Be a High Probability Thinker and repetitively trade on high probability setups.

Action-3: Be your own analyst and decide independent from what you see on your charts: Trade what you see!

Action-4: Stay engaged, keep your money working for you by establishing an opportunity finder, which guides you to favorable trade setups.

Action-5: Know and apply trade adjustment methods to stack the odds in your favor.

You have two choices now: Develop all of this on your own or come on board with a market proven mentorship program: NeverLossTrading.

We are offering multiple mentorship and suite them to your individual wants and needs. To ensure best applicability all our teaching sessions are individually held and recorded for you.

Here are some chart examples for the different NLT Concepts that can also be combined:

NLT HF-Day Trading Example for 30-Year Bond Futures on a 4-Hour Chart

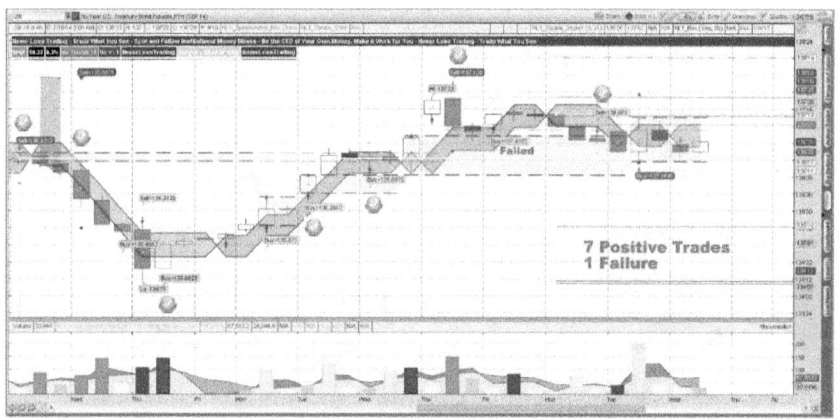

NLT IncomeGenerator Chart for the Emini S&P 500 Futures on a 30-Minute Chart

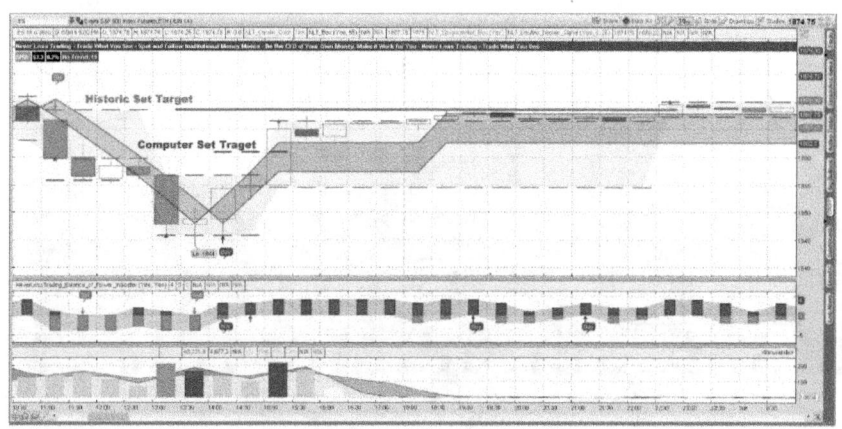

NLT Swing Point Trading, AMGN on a Daily Chart

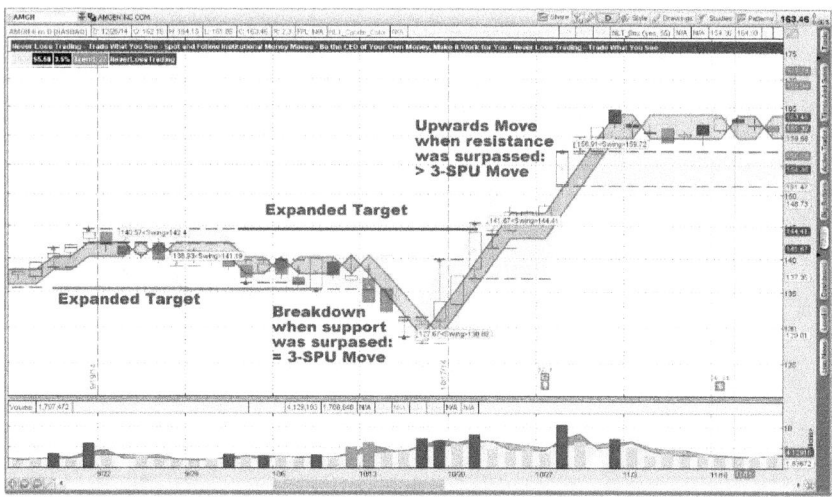

TradeColors.com Chart for Gold Futures: One Contract

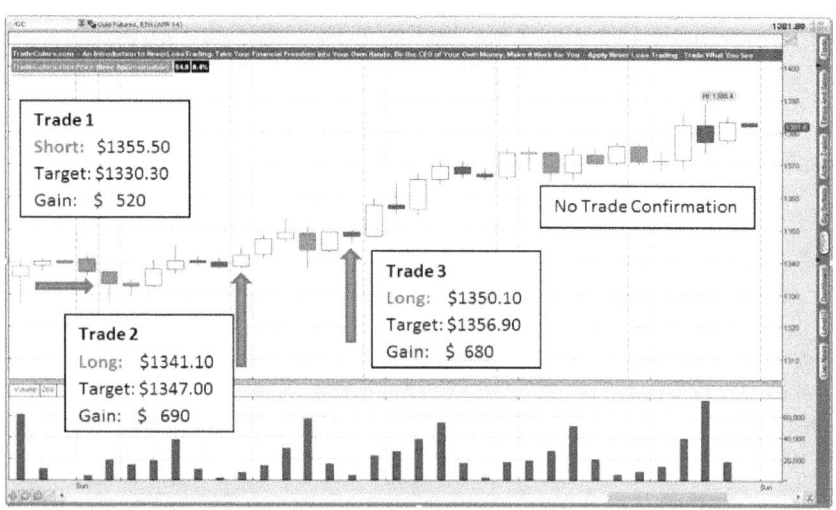

TradeColors.com is our basic program. If you decided to start with this, we will allow you for a later upgrade to NLT Top-Line or NLT HF Trading, acknowledging every dollar you spent on tuition.

A TradeColors.com mentorship includes:

The NLT Candle Color Indicator

4-Hours of Individual Training

1-Month Questions Answered

Software Installed (1 hour)

50 Pages of Documentation

30-Days Free Alerts

$2,497 (Introductory Offer)

Fully REFUNDABLE on Upgrades

The NLT Top-Line Mentorship includes:

About 20 Indicators (incl. Candle Color)

20-Hours of Individual Training (flexible)

6-Month Mentorship (2 hours/month)

Software Installed (5-7 hours)

180 – 300 Pages of Documentation

90-Days Free Report

Watch Lists and/or Scanners (Installed)

$9,997 (one-time payment or cooperation with our financing partner PayPal)

Take the opportunity and schedule your individual consulting hour:

Call: +1 866 455 4520 or contact@NeverLossTrading.com

We are looking forward to hearing back from you.

Good trading,

Thomas Barmann

NeverLossTrading

A Division of Nobel Living, LLC

401 E. Las Olas Blvd. – Suite 1400

Fort Lauderdale, FL 33301

Disclaimer

Chapter 16 - Harnessing the Power of the Market Scanner and Average Range Report by Gail Mercer

One of the most frustrating aspects of trading, is sitting around waiting on the setup. However, by combining the powers of the THD indicators with the Market Scanner, a trader is no longer glued to his (or her) computer screens.

For example, here is a snapshot of the Market Scanner with the THD indicators for Thursday, May 14 2015 at 7:30 am ET.

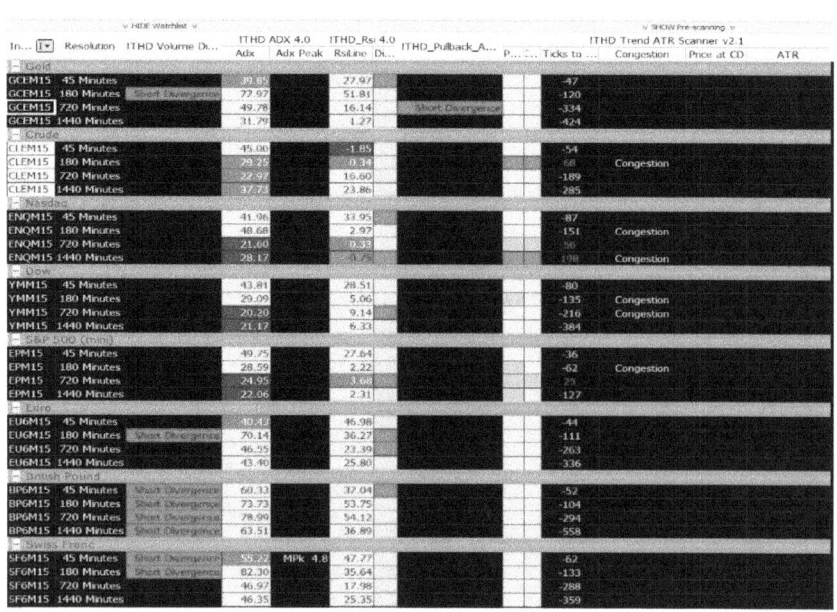

While at first glance, the window may seem overwhelming, let's break it down by column.

The first two column identify the symbols and the timeframes that we are monitoring with the indicators.

The next column is the THD Volume Divergence indicator and identifies when there is volume divergence in the trend. This information easily identifies when to exercise caution in entering the trend, i.e. if you are in a long position on Gold you may want to consider locking in profits as the trend is showing a short divergence (possible reversal), which is a sign of trend weakness.

The next column is the THD ADX indicator. Anytime the ADX column is above 70, a retracement back to the ATR is anticipated. If the background color of this column is blue, expect a downward movement. If the background color is red, expect an upward movement. Additionally, the next column identifies if a magenta peak is occurring (retracement to ATR is imminent).

After the column showing the magenta peak, the THD RSI indicator identifies overbought and oversold conditions, as well. A value greater than 50 is considered to be overbought or oversold. Again, if blue, it is overbought or, if red, is oversold. If the column next to the RSI value is red, then there is divergence on the RSI.

Before we proceed, let's review the markets that are showing divergences:

• Gold

O Short Divergence on the 180 minute timeframe
O Overbought on the ADX (value at 77.97)
O Overbought on the RSI (value at 51.81)

• Euro

O Short Divergence on the 180 minute timeframe
O Overbought on the ADX (value at 70.14)
O RSI is only at 36 but showing divergence (red column next to the RSI value)

• British Pound

O Short Divergence on all timeframes
O Overbought on ADX, both the 180 and 720 minute timeframes (values at 73.73 and 78.99)
O Overbought on RSI, both the 180 and 720 minute timeframes (values at 53.75 and 54.12)

• Swiss Franc

O Short Divergence on 45 and 180 minute timeframes
O Magenta peak on 45 minute timeframe (MPk 4.8)
O Overbought ADX on 180 minute timeframe (value at 82.30)

Identifying these conditions, prior to the US Market opening, signals that the market may retrace. But how far will the retracements go? While we could look at each individual charts and plot Fibonacci lines, we can easily identify "how much" retracement is expected by simply using the THD Trend ATR Scanner tools.

The first column under the THD Trend ATR Scanner v2.1 shows the previous trend color, followed by the current trend color. The next column tells us "how much" of a retracement is likely to occur. Using this information, combined with the information above we can anticipate the following:

• Gold – 120 tick retracement
• Euro – 111 tick retracement
• British Pound – 104 tick retracement
• Swiss Franc – 133 tick retracement

And what happened on these markets? By 8am the next morning, we saw the following movement:

• Gold – 100 tick downward movement.
• Euro – 94 pips downward movement.
• British Pound – 88 pips downward movement.
• Swiss Franc – 128 pips downward movement.

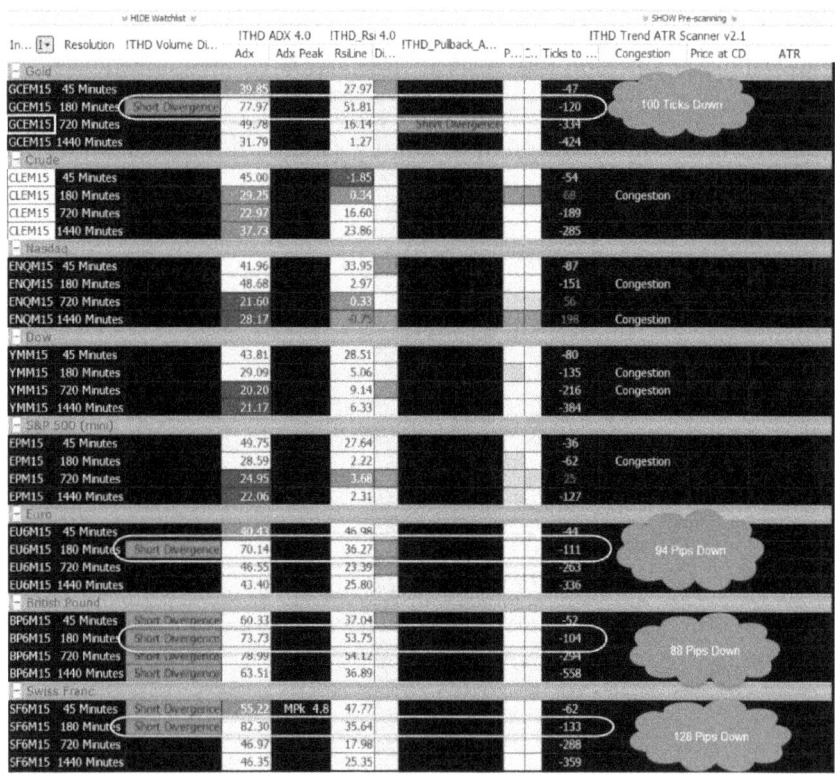

And, we could anticipate that these trades would take on average 24 hours to work in our favor. Why? Using the charts below, the average range (high minus low) for a 24 hour period on these markets are:

- Gold – 190 ticks
- Euro – 138 pips
- British Pound – 136 pips
- Swiss Franc – 145 pips

	2006	2007	2008	2009	2010	2011	2012	2013	2014	2015
AUDUSD	63	89	157	141	121	163	90	93	74	101
EURUSD	105	92	83	185	169	150	158	97	75	138
GBPUSD	135	131	229	224	161	141	97	111	88	136
USDCAD	83	92	155	165	112	96	64	60	68	133
USDCHF	106	85	151	137	116	119	78	79	58	145
USDJPY	94	100	149	125	89	66	57	107	74	102

	2006	2007	2008	2009	2010	2011	2012	2013	2014	2015
GC	9	12	26	20	19	31	23	26	17	19
CL	1.2	2.03	4.33	2.72	2.18	3.05	2.23	1.81	1.78	2.56
YM	106	160	311	183	154	207	149	140	161	227
ES	13	20	36	22	18	24	17	17	20	26
NQ	26	32	56	34	35	47	38	35	49	59

Using the charts below which measure the average range for each sixty minute period, we can identify that the most movement during a sixty minute period, for May, on each of these markets are:

• Gold – between 8 am to 9 am then 9 am to10 am
• Euro – between 10 am and 11 am then 3 am to 4 am
• British Pound – between 4 am and 5 am then 10 am to 11 am
• Swiss Franc - between 8 am to 9 am and 10 am to 11 am

Gold (Points, 10 ticks equals 1 point)											
	Jan	Feb	Mar	Apr	May	Jun	Jul	Aug	Sep	Oct	Nov	Dec
12:00 AM	1.89	1.76	2.01	1.65	1.82	1.43	1.65	1.34	1.74	2.06	3.44	2.37
1:00 AM	2.91	2.38	1.83	1.69	1.29	1.76	1.76	1.39	1.63	1.63	3.78	2.61
2:00 AM	2.94	2.70	2.94	2.42	2.00	1.89	2.33	1.93	2.34	2.60	3.93	3.03
3:00 AM	3.50	2.78	3.37	3.64	2.86	2.63	3.50	2.85	3.27	3.08	4.11	3.38
4:00 AM	4.17	3.72	3.37	3.26	3.25	2.84	2.64	2.80	2.64	4.23	4.35	4.33
5:00 AM	4.05	3.28	3.93	3.39	2.60	2.41	2.31	2.37	2.94	2.97	3.14	4.14
6:00 AM	3.40	3.39	3.11	2.99	2.56	2.65	2.64	1.99	2.56	2.96	3.81	4.50
7:00 AM	3.60	2.78	2.87	2.93	2.67	2.16	2.15	2.65	3.48	2.33	3.99	3.51
8:00 AM	4.45	4.17	3.38	3.76	2.81	2.68	3.00	2.78	3.37	3.19	3.73	4.90
9:00 AM	7.74	6.42	6.17	6.60	7.24	5.79	5.75	6.58	4.95	6.35	6.66	7.76
10:00 AM	6.11	5.88	5.67	5.45	4.05	4.28	5.05	3.84	5.25	5.46	5.09	6.85
11:00 AM	6.99	6.27	5.47	5.05	5.30	4.22	4.73	4.73	4.81	4.69	6.72	7.63
12:00 PM	5.03	4.16	4.22	3.47	3.81	2.70	4.19	3.32	3.67	3.51	5.32	5.44
1:00 PM	3.24	3.26	3.64	2.81	2.67	2.94	2.67	2.31	2.86	3.23	5.73	4.43
2:00 PM	4.19	3.40	3.01	2.90	2.34	2.44	2.49	2.50	2.50	2.55	3.99	4.03
3:00 PM	3.98	3.17	3.36	2.54	2.22	2.30	2.45	2.08	2.39	2.88	4.24	4.72
4:00 PM	3.36	2.92	2.75	2.22	1.94	2.17	2.58	2.05	3.07	2.55	3.53	3.50
5:00 PM	2.36	2.03	2.09	1.50	1.46	1.65	1.50	1.49	1.78	1.99	2.46	2.47
5:15 PM	1.08	1.05	0.91	0.88	0.92	0.98	0.80	0.80	0.89	0.93	1.12	1.09
7:00 PM	3.37	2.62	2.50	2.14	2.16	1.88	2.27	1.38	2.19	2.78	4.39	3.22
8:00 PM	2.96	2.52	2.12	1.69	1.39	1.47	1.55	1.14	1.62	1.78	2.69	2.76
9:00 PM	3.89	3.44	2.78	2.46	2.27	1.63	1.65	1.64	2.00	2.28	4.04	3.86
10:00 PM	2.78	2.26	4.11	3.13	2.79	3.03	2.41	1.81	3.35	2.85	2.46	2.27
11:00 PM	2.30	1.84	2.49	2.14	1.59	1.85	1.83	1.65	2.27	1.98	2.69	1.95

EURUSD											
	Jan	Feb	Mar	Apr	May	Jun	Jul	Aug	Sep	Oct	Nov	Dec
12:00 AM	9	6	10	7	4	4	3	5	8	10	10	9
1:00 AM	11	8	10	7	4	4	4	5	7	9	10	9
2:00 AM	14	12	12	9	6	6	5	6	9	11	12	12
3:00 AM	21	20	17	18	12	13	10	14	16	21	20	23
4:00 AM	30	23	30	24	16	15	14	15	17	24	28	25
5:00 AM	29	23	28	19	15	16	13	13	18	25	23	22
6:00 AM	24	21	24	18	12	14	10	14	16	25	20	19
7:00 AM	24	18	25	16	14	12	8	11	14	18	18	18
8:00 AM	25	21	23	17	12	16	8	10	18	21	15	19
9:00 AM	37	32	37	32	21	24	16	21	24	41	35	33
10:00 AM	33	26	33	27	15	19	14	16	23	31	29	25
11:00 AM	33	27	30	27	22	20	14	21	25	29	30	29
12:00 PM	23	22	26	19	11	13	9	14	20	23	23	23
1:00 PM	20	20	24	14	9	10	8	10	16	19	16	20
2:00 PM	15	16	24	13	9	11	7	9	14	17	18	16
3:00 PM	18	15	21	14	8	10	8	9	13	23	16	20
4:00 PM	14	13	14	11	6	7	4	6	13	18	10	13
4:59 PM	12	11	15	8	5	6	4	5	7	13	7	8
6:00 PM	13	9	11	6	5	4	3	5	7	9	9	8
7:00 PM	12	9	10	6	3	4	3	4	7	9	9	12
8:00 PM	16	11	11	7	4	5	4	4	7	11	17	11
9:00 PM	15	10	14	13	8	7	5	7	9	14	13	12
10:00 PM	11	10	13	9	6	7	5	8	11	14	13	9
11:00 PM	10	9	11	9	6	5	5	6	9	11	11	9

GBPUSD

	Jan	Feb	Mar	Apr	May	Jun	Jul	Aug	Sep	Oct	Nov	Dec
12:00 AM	10	8	10	9	6	6	4	7	13	12	10	10
1:00 AM	11	9	11	8	5	5	6	5	12	10	12	9
2:00 AM	13	14	12	11	8	8	6	8	17	12	14	13
3:00 AM	26	25	19	18	15	16	14	14	28	27	21	25
4:00 AM	31	29	29	23	19	15	15	13	25	27	27	29
5:00 AM	40	35	30	33	28	27	25	25	35	35	34	35
6:00 AM	26	29	33	20	16	19	15	19	25	27	30	24
7:00 AM	26	22	26	21	16	15	13	14	23	22	23	26
8:00 AM	28	24	26	20	16	15	13	15	22	21	20	25
9:00 AM	40	31	36	33	21	20	20	17	30	37	30	31
10:00 AM	32	26	37	26	17	17	16	13	28	31	30	29
11:00 AM	35	36	32	26	20	19	17	17	27	31	29	35
12:00 PM	27	26	29	19	14	14	13	12	27	25	24	26
1:00 PM	19	20	26	16	10	13	9	10	22	18	18	20
2:00 PM	17	18	23	14	9	12	9	8	17	21	19	16
3:00 PM	19	17	24	17	10	11	10	9	19	25	15	22
4:00 PM	15	13	17	11	7	10	7	8	16	20	11	17
4:59 PM	14	12	17	10	7	12	6	7	13	13	9	12
6:00 PM	16	12	12	8	6	7	5	6	17	11	13	12
7:00 PM	12	11	11	7	5	6	5	5	13	12	10	13
8:00 PM	15	13	12	8	4	7	6	6	12	13	18	15
9:00 PM	15	12	14	14	8	9	8	9	18	17	13	13
10:00 PM	11	11	13	11	7	8	7	9	17	14	15	11
11:00 PM	11	10	11	9	7	7	6	7	15	12	12	8

USDCHF

	Jan	Feb	Mar	Apr	May	Jun	Jul	Aug	Sep	Oct	Nov	Dec
12:00 AM	12	8	9	5	3	4	2	4	6	8	8	7
1:00 AM	14	9	8	6	3	3	3	3	6	7	7	7
2:00 AM	18	12	8	7	4	4	3	5	7	9	9	11
3:00 AM	26	20	15	12	9	9	7	10	13	15	16	21
4:00 AM	34	24	23	18	13	11	10	11	15	19	23	21
5:00 AM	31	21	23	16	11	11	9	10	14	19	17	17
6:00 AM	27	19	20	14	9	10	7	11	12	19	15	15
7:00 AM	28	16	21	13	10	9	6	8	12	15	15	15
8:00 AM	26	18	17	14	8	12	6	7	13	16	13	15
9:00 AM	36	27	28	24	16	17	12	17	19	32	27	27
10:00 AM	38	23	24	22	12	14	11	12	18	25	23	20
11:00 AM	41	24	26	21	16	16	11	16	20	24	24	24
12:00 PM	30	22	24	16	9	10	7	11	15	18	19	19
1:00 PM	25	17	20	12	7	8	6	8	13	15	13	16
2:00 PM	22	17	18	12	7	9	5	7	11	13	14	13
3:00 PM	24	14	18	11	6	8	6	7	10	18	13	16
4:00 PM	17	12	14	9	5	5	3	4	10	13	8	11
4:59 PM	15	10	14	7	4	4	3	4	6	10	6	7
6:00 PM	16	9	10	6	3	3	3	4	6	7	7	6
7:00 PM	13	9	10	5	2	3	2	3	5	7	7	9
8:00 PM	16	11	8	5	3	3	3	3	6	9	13	9
9:00 PM	14	11	12	9	5	5	4	5	7	10	10	10
10:00 PM	15	11	10	7	4	5	4	6	9	10	10	8
11:00 PM	11	9	9	7	3	4	3	5	7	8	8	7

Since we are anticipating over 100 ticks (or pips) of movement, we can deduce that our trades need to capture both the London and US sessions (or a 24 hour period).

Then on Friday morning, 5/15/15, the Market Scanner showed that the indices had short divergence and the higher timeframes were overbought.

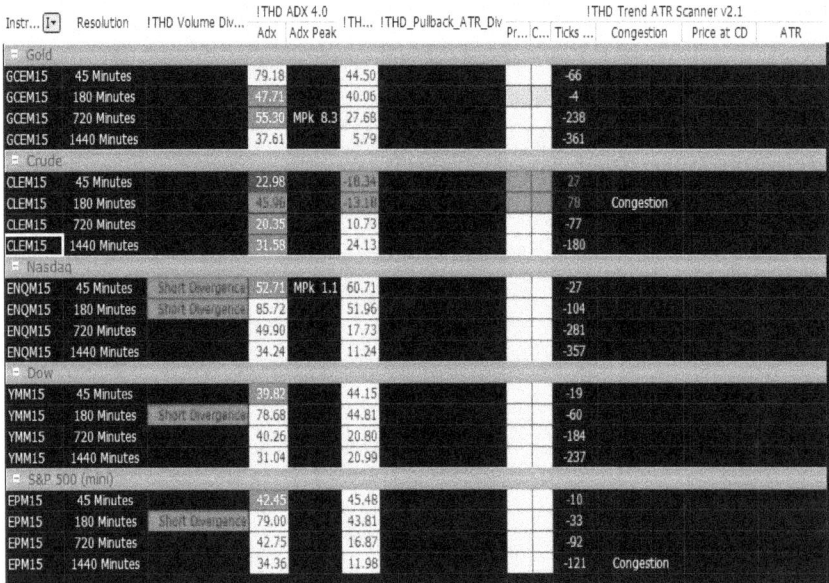

Instr...	Resolution	!THD Volume Div...	!THD ADX 4.0 Adx	Adx Peak	!TH...	!THD_Pullback_ATR_Div	Pr...	C...	Ticks ...	Congestion	Price at CD	ATR
Gold												
GCEM15	45 Minutes		79.18		44.50				-66			
GCEM15	180 Minutes		47.71		40.06				-4			
GCEM15	720 Minutes		55.30	MPk 8.3	27.68				-238			
GCEM15	1440 Minutes		37.61		5.79				-361			
Crude												
CLEM15	45 Minutes		22.98		-10.34				27			
CLEM15	180 Minutes		45.96		-13.10				78	Congestion		
CLEM15	720 Minutes		20.35		10.73				-77			
CLEM15	1440 Minutes		31.58		24.13				-180			
Nasdaq												
ENQM15	45 Minutes	Short Divergence	52.71	MPk 1.1	60.71				-27			
ENQM15	180 Minutes	Short Divergence	85.72		51.96				-104			
ENQM15	720 Minutes		49.90		17.73				-281			
ENQM15	1440 Minutes		34.24		11.24				-357			
Dow												
YMM15	45 Minutes		39.82		44.15				-19			
YMM15	180 Minutes	Short Divergence	78.68		44.81				-60			
YMM15	720 Minutes		40.26		20.80				-184			
YMM15	1440 Minutes		31.04		20.99				-237			
S&P 500 (mini)												
EPM15	45 Minutes		42.45		45.48				-10			
EPM15	180 Minutes	Short Divergence	79.00		43.81				-33			
EPM15	720 Minutes		42.75		16.87				-92			
EPM15	1440 Minutes		34.36		11.98				-121	Congestion		

!THD Trend ATR Scanner v2.1

By going down to a 12 minute chart, trades were entered as price retraced back to the red plus sign (ATR) on diverging volume (highlighted with red line).

The Dow resulted in a fifty-three point gain (expecting sixty points of movement).

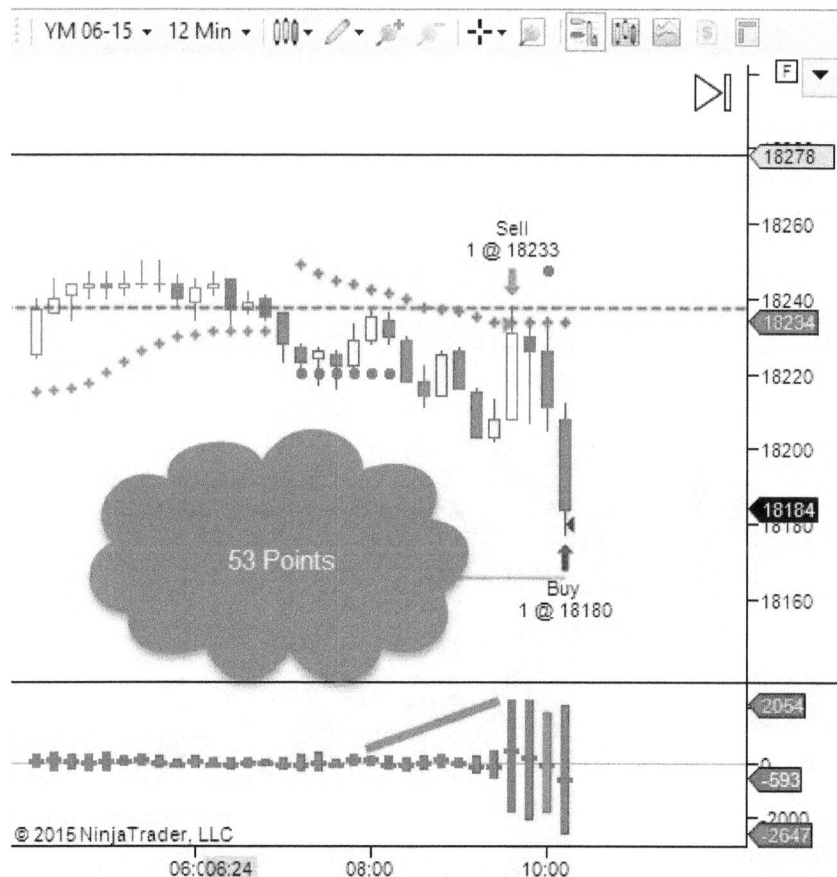

Dow Trade

The Nasdaq trade resulted in a twenty point gain for eighty ticks (expecting one hundred and two ticks).

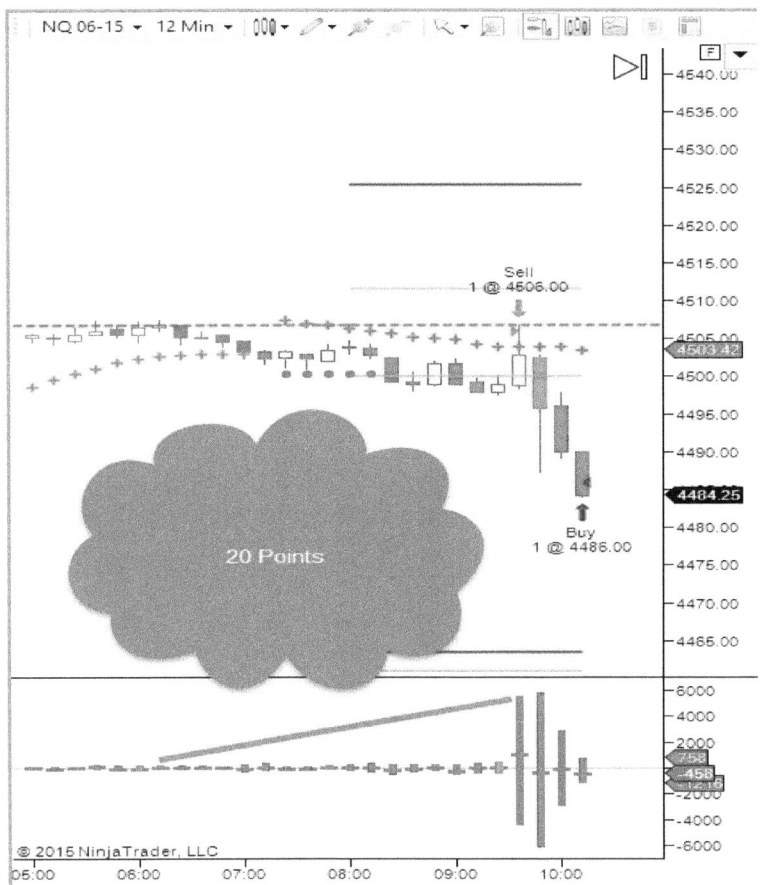

Nasdaq Trade

By utilizing the powers of the THD indicators with the Market Scanner and combining the "how much" a market will move on average statistics, we can easily identify our trade opportunities in advance and identify "how long" our trades will take to achieve their potential profit targets. The only decision remaining is whether to do small intraday trades or an overnight trade to capture the profits or even a combination of the two methods.

Since we have email alerts, visual alerts and audio alerts programmed into these Scanner indicators, we no longer have to be glued to the computer screen. Instead, we can simply setup the alerts and know exactly when we need to check our markets.

You can download the free Market Volatility Report by visiting clicking here. Additionally, you can contact Gail at gm@tradershelpdesk.com or visit our website at www.TradersHelpDesk.com

Chapter 17 – Stop Guessing! By Gerard P. Reynaud

The moment you realize you just missed a good trade setup, it's the moment your emotions start flowing like sweat down your head. What coulda', shoulda', woulda' happened if you had you just hit the button on the mouse?

Oh well... But then it happens again, you see a good trade setup and you realize you missed it again! This time, however, you blame it on the phone, the wife, the kids or the cat.

You say to yourself - it's no big deal. There's another setup just around the corner.

Next instance you execute and enter the trade. Good. You pushed yourself to finally pulling the trigger. And you did. And then what happened? Did you exit the trade early? Did you move your stop? Did you achieve your profit targets? Did you lose more than expected? Finally, you realized –again- that it may have been better to miss the trade. You found yourself paying the broker, and possibly ended up with a mediocre out come.

Friends, we have all been there and we've all done that. It's part of the learning curve.

Trading is an activity that requires to reverse-program our thinking process and unless we do that, it will get the best out of all human emotions every time. I do not know any good traders who don't check the 'emotions' at the door before coming into their trading desks. But how can you reverse-program ourselves to achieve better outcomes? Only by the power exercised from a 100% objective rule-based approach.

In my career as a trader and a trading coach, I've seen the best rule-based systems wrecked by inexperienced traders. A wise trader once said, I could publish my entire system in the front page of the news paper for the whole world to replicate, and I bet you will not even come close to reproducing my results".

It's a pretty heavy statement. But true. The system is only the means by which we can approach the markets, but the execution is left to the trader which has a greater statistical probability of messing everything up, even if a great system is in place.

So we have two parts of the equation; the system and the trader.

Let's talk about the system and its importance.

Unless you have a system that relies only on objective rule-based signals for your executions, you will not find success in trading in the long term.

When most aspiring traders come to me, one of the first things I hear is, "I've tried 4-5 different systems over the last few years and none of them produced the results I thought they were capable of". To which my answer is always the same –"Did your system involved 100% objective rule-based signals from the start'?

So, unless that's your starting approach, you will only find yourself struggling for a long time, and your equity curve will continue to suffer as much as you. I'm sorry to cut through the bad news so bluntly, but a little candor goes a long way.

The good news, is there is help and there is a solution. Even in the most manipulated environments, successful trading for the beginner retail trader is possible.

The other thing that I find interesting when I talk to newbie traders is that most of them believe their first systems had an overwhelming chance of success. Most systems on the Internet sell for stratospheric amounts claiming 80 or 90% success rate...

The best systems of statistical-proven success over the long haul are only able to achieve an average of 65-70% winning rate though all market conditions. That means periods of high and low volatility as well as heavy rallies. Keep in mind that most systems win more and can generate 90% success returns on strong trending/high volatility environments, if executed properly. But these occurrences are rare. So, once again, a little candor goes along way.

The best way to position one self into a territory that will allow you to tackle your first years a starting trader without the pitfalls of big draw downs and emotional disfunction is to abide yourself to a proven system with objective rules.

Have you found one yet? One of the most common ways that investors and traders measure the potential results of any given trading system is through back testing. While back testing is always a good option to see how any given system could have potentially performed on any given market, it also has a lot of limitations. The first one, being that past performance is absolutely not indicative of future performance. By far the best way to put a system to the test is to forward-test it in present conditions utilizing a virtual or simulator account.

Many find the art of trading to be extremely hard to manage. It is true that a big majority has failed and will fail at it. But let's make a big distinction here. Just in the same way that any driver will fail to stop his/her automobile at the next light without brakes, traders fail at this because of a lack objective rule-based signals, discipline and mentoring. Think you can figure out an Algebra textbook by yourself? Trading is no different.

After that, the last resource is to think an automated trading machine will do the trick. You'll probably remember Capt. "Sully". He was the pilot that landed the US Airways flight safely in the Hudson River a few years ago, without any casualties, and became an immediate national hero. He expressed his opinion about technology, auto pilots and letting airplanes fly all through technology. This is particularly interesting since the world of trading is seeing its own share of HFT, computerized systems and auto traders, most of which attract the likes of beginner traders. Here's what he said about it:

"Technology has its strengths and weaknesses. For example, it is superior to humans in its ability to consistently monitor conditions over an extended period of time, which is why technology is essential in screening passengers before they board a flight. Yet in spite of technology's continuously improving reliability, anyone who doubts that it can fail at the most inopportune time has likely never used a computer." The more layers are piled into increasingly complex systems, the more failure paths we introduce. We've learned that automation does not eliminate errors. Rather, it changes the nature of the errors that are made, and it makes possible new kinds of errors."

On the illustrations below, you will see a simple trading system that my team and I designed over the last few years and that it has proven to work over 70% of time in any market condition. Figure 1 will show you the tools for the trade and our proprietary set of indicators by which my team and I base our rule-entry signals.

Figure 2 will show you and add-on indicator that will help you with signal recognition that will never fail in generating a signal based on, you guessed it right, our objective rule-based signals.

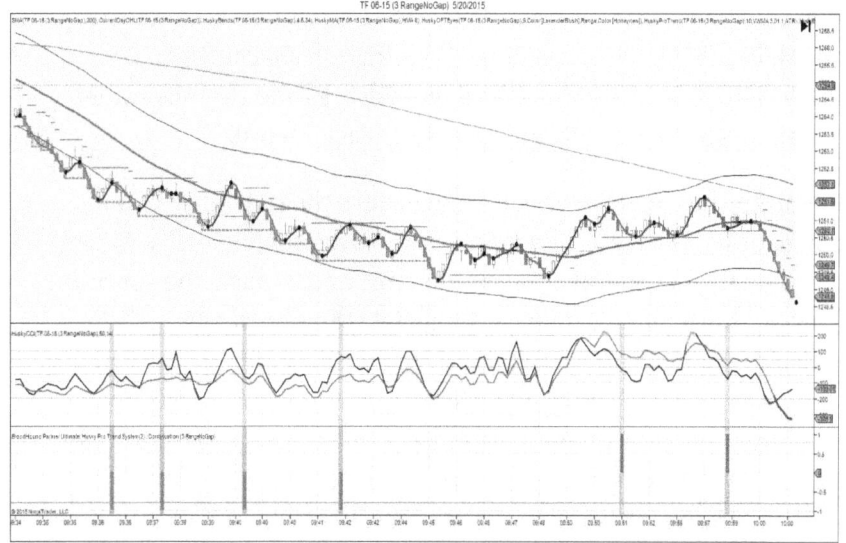

So forget about trying to guess where the market will go next. No body knows. Our job as traders is to abide by a set of proven rules over time, not lose money and control our risk. Successful trading is possible. Don't miss our video presentation on how our system and signal generation indicators work. Stop guessing, and put the power of profits by your side.

Happy Trading!

Gerard P. Reynaud

President/Founder

Tradermakers.com

Gerard P. Reynaud is the Founder and Senior Trader at InverPro Capital, Inc, and head coach at the well-known coaching firm, TraderMakers. A 15-year professional Futures and Options trader with an extensive trading and investing track record.

CHAPTER 18 – TRADING WITH KNOWN PROBABILITIES BY ROB MITCHELL

One thing stands head and shoulders above the rest when it comes to trading; probability!

For traders, knowing the probability that certain events will occur within certain limits is of value on a variety of levels. One, it prevents psychological traps. For example, if I know there is an 80% probability we are going 15 ticks higher and I end up being wrong, I know I made the correct decision. There is no mental trap. If I trade into a situation that is random, and I lose, then I know I made the wrong decision. I knew in advance there was a good chance of being wrong. If I do not know the probability however, I have no way no way of knowing I am making the correct decision and no way of correcting the accuracy of my trading. Worse yet, I have no way of learning. When I trade with known probabilities, I have a framework for improving my trading. So, why take random 50% probability trades when there are 80 and 90% probability trades going on all day.

Beyond basic psychological factors is the probability itself. Nate Silver in his recent book, "The Signal and the Noise", discusses these kinds of probability scenarios within the context of everything from weather, earthquakes, poker and sports betting. He talks about one professional sports gambler who makes several million dollars a year betting on sports. What is interesting about this is he operates on a 4% margin. In other words, he wins 54% of the time. Many of the probabilities we deal with in trading can be in the 80-90% area; 30-40% better than random (50% is random so, 80% - 50% is a 30% advantage)!

How do we find and compute such probabilities? The way you will typically see probabilities in trading is when they are associated with trading systems. Often these are back tests. In this scenario, there is a complicated rule set that identifies certain non-direct patterns in the price data that may win or lose a certain percentage of the time. The kinds of probabilities we are referring to here are direct probabilities. They may have to do with price action around recent highs or lows, or they may have to do with sequencing of waves. Other patterns might include range extensions or targeting types of computations. Some of these probabilities happen every day and the levels are hit as much as 98% of the time. When we do this form of analysis, we collect statistics on large amounts of data and occurrences and reduce them to simple rules of thumb so they are easy to remember, learn and use. Let's take a look at a structure we call the Three Period Probability Walk.

The Three Period Probability Walk looks at where a sequence of bars begins and ends. This works in any reasonably volatile market. Let's take Crude Oil for example, arguably the market with the most opportunity in it for intraday traders. Most traders know you get good movement off the open in pit traded markets but what are the probabilities associated with this extension? In the following table, A is the first 30 minutes of the day, B is the second and C is the third. After tabulating this data we can see that the first period of this sequence is the high or low 82% of the time. This means movements away from this area are highprobability. The range for this interval is 95 ticks or $950 per contract in crude oil with a standard deviation of 38 ticks. This simply means a normal market extends here from 57 to 133 ticks about 68% of the time. Of course the overall potential here is astounding and the amount of risk, if given the tools to manage it (see below for more on management), is about 15 ticks or so. This means every morning there is an opportunity to the tune of a minimum of 3.8:1 or, 3.8 times profit to risk in this market. You may not be able to capture all of that (some days are more and some days are less) but, by knowing this statistic, we can plan, organize and implement our trades within the given probability framework. It gets better though....

A, B, C
71% says C takes out both A&B
62% says B is in the middle
82% says A is one end of it
Average Range 95 ticks
Standard Deviation 38 ticks
** (A, B & C are the first three 30 minute periods)

There are other statistics in the table we can use that are well above random (>50%). But there are even more simple, rule of thumb, statistics we can use. First let's summarize what we have covered so far. The Crude Oil market will move 95 ticks on average off the open each day in the first 1.5 hours. The second 30 minute period is in the middle, meaning the whole first 1.5 hours is a trend (higher highs and lows or, lower lows and highs all the way) 62% of the time. The third period will exceed both the first two 71% of the time (see the table above).

Another rule of thumb we also know is, how likely it is we will exceed the previous period by, and how much and with what probability. This statistic might read something like, B, or the second 30 minute period will take out the first 30 minute period (A) 86% of the time. Further, it will take it out by more than 5 ticks 83% of the time and goes more than 20 ticks 36% of the time (see table below). This statistic works in a tighter framework than the larger scaled Three Bar Probability Walk. So what you get is high probability statistics working within a framework of other high probability statistics. As this unfolds, the market begins to tell a story. With some practice you can even begin to predict different shapes the market will form in to. Figuring out this ongoing story is fun. It is like solving a puzzle and it makes trading feel like you are playing while trading; an experience few traders ever get to feel.

	B
Avg Extension	0.20
>.05	83%
>.1	67%
>.15	48%
>.2	36%
>.25	28%
>.3	21%
>.35	17%
>.4	14%
>.45	12%
>.5	10%

As you practice trading within this framework, what happens is you begin to develop an intuitive understanding of the way the market works. But, it is not just any intuition, it is intuition based on statistical facts. So what happens is your belief system comes into alignment with what is real in your traded market.

Trading is like a profession. Doctors practice medicine. Lawyers practice law. Traders practice trading. So you are always developing your skill and knowledge. If you have a way of evaluating your outcomes as you go, you have a way of developing an excellent skill set. If you do not have a mechanism for this you will likely be in the group of the 95% of traders who fail.

It is still important that traders carefully manage the risk of their trades. In the intraday frames there are a couple different ways the market might unfold as a trade develops toward the statistic. One, it can chop or grind its way there. Some days are golden and you get immediate follow through or what I call run away trades. So, how do you manage the risk? It is best to have a trading system that operates on market structure and price action. This way you have a way of managing both the above mentioned scenarios. For this, we use the Smart Patterns Trading System from IndicatorSmart.com (the system we also use at OilTradingRoom.com). This system is designed from the bottom up. First, the system organizes the price data into bars that are based on specific structures or price bars based on order flow; the most fundamental level of analysis. This help to stack things in your favor for having efficient, manageable entries or trade triggers. Next, the system has a position management tool for helping you to manage your trade in a trend.

This "bottom up" structure gives you the tools you need to trade towards larger scale targets that can be a substantial distance away (analysis from the "top down"). Many days you will be able to identify targets with high probability that are quite large with respect to the risk that you take as we originally described in this article. With the higher time frame probabilities operating at a larger scale and the system functioning to control and manage risk all the way down into the order flow level, you have a complete system for finding high levels of opportunity each trading day.

Rob Mitchell is a Robbins World Cup Champion trader. He teaches trading at OilTradingRoom.com and provides trading solutions for traders at all levels through IndicatorSmart.com.

Copyright

ABOUT THE AUTHOR

Larry Jacobs has a B.S. and Master's Degree in Business and has been editor of Traders World Magazine since 1988. It's a leading financial magazine which has both classical and modern technical analysis articles as well as reviews of the latest trading books, trading computer hardware and software.

He also has written dozens of articles on how to setup your home trading office and how to get the right trading computer.

He is author of several trading books including Gann Masters, Gann Masters II, Gann Master Charts Unveiled, Patterns and Ellipses and W. D. Gann in Real Time Trading. Gann Masters was so popular it was recently translated in to Italian.

He has reviewed almost every trading software program available and has interviewed and talked to the many of leading traders of the world.

He won the World Cup Championship of Stock Trading® in 2001.

Disclaimer

All trading involves risk. Leveraged trading has large potential rewards, but also large potential risk. Be aware and accept this risk before trading. Never trade with money you cannot afford to lose. All forecasting is based on past performance and past performance of any trading methodology is no guarantee of future results. No "safe" trading system has ever been devised and no one can guarantee profits or freedom from loss. No representation is being made that any account will achieve profits or losses similar to those discussed. There is no guarantee that, even with the best advice available, you will become a successful trader because not everyone has what it takes to be a successful trader. The trading strategies discussed may be unsuitable for you depending upon your specific investment objectives and financial position. You must make your own investment decisions in light of your own investment objectives, risk profile, and circumstances. Use independent advisors as you believe necessary. Therefore, the information provided herein is not intended to be specific advice as to whether you should engage in a particular trading strategy or buy, sell, or hold any financial product. Margin requirements, tax considerations, commissions, and other transaction costs may significantly affect the economic consequences of the trading strategies or transactions discussed and you should review such requirements with your own legal, tax and financial advisors. Before engaging in such trading activities, you should understand the nature and extent of your rights and obligations and be aware of the risks involved. All testimonials are unsolicited and are potentially non-representative of all clients. Halliker's,Inc. dba

withstand losses (and incur account drawdowns) or to adhere to a particular trading program in spite of trading loses are important issues which can also adversely affect actual trading results. There are numerous other factors related to the markets in general or to the implementation of any specific trading program, method or system, which cannot be completely taken into consideration with hypothetical performance results and will affect trading results and your P/L.

Trading Disclaimer:

Futures and forex trading have large potential rewards, but also large potential risk. You must be aware of the risks and be willing to accept them in order to invest in the futures and options markets. Don't trade with money you can't afford to lose. This letter is neither a solicitation nor an offer to Buy/Sell futures or options. No representation is being made that any account will or is likely to achieve profits or losses similar to those discussed on this letter. The past performance of any trading system or methodology is not necessarily indicative of future results. Trading foreign currencies is a challenging and potentially profitable opportunity for educated and experienced investors. However, before deciding to participate in the Forex market, you should carefully consider your investment objectives, level of experience and risk appetite. Most importantly, do not invest money you cannot afford to lose. There is considerable exposure to risk in any foreign exchange transaction. Any transaction involving currencies involves risks including, but not limited to, the potential for changing political and/or economic conditions that may substantially affect the price or liquidity of a currency.

OTHER TRADERS WORLD BOOKS

Guide to Successful Online Trading: Secrets from the Pros

http://www.amazon.com/Guide-Successful-Online-Trading-Secrets-ebook/dp/B00QOBED34

This is one of the finest trading books you'll ever see about trading. The reason is that it comes from a group of expert pro traders with multiple years of experience.

Trading as you know is extremely difficult. It is estimated that 90% of traders lose money in the markets. To help you overcome this statistic, the pro traders in this book give you their ideas on trading with some of the best trading methods ever developed through their long time experience. By reading about these trading methods and implementing them in the markets you will then have a chance to then join the ranks of the 10% of the successful traders.

The traders in this book have through experience the right attitude and employ a combination of technical analysis principles and strategies to be successful. You can develop these also.

Trading is one of the best ways to make money. Apply the trading methods in this book and treat it as a business. The purpose of this book is to help you be successful in trading.

From this book you will get all the strategies, Indicators and trading methods that you need to make big profits in the markets.

This book gives you:

1) Audio/Visual Links to presentations from pro traders

2) The best strategies that the professional traders are using now

3) The broad perspective you need in today's difficult markets

4) The Exact tools that you need to make profitable trading decisions

5) The finest trading education

I wish to express my appreciation to all the writers in this book who made the book possible. They have spent many hours of their time and hard work in writing their section of the book and the putting together their video presentation for the online expo.

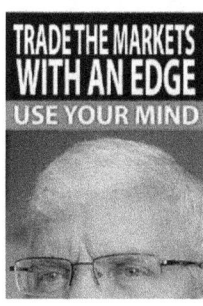

Trade the Markets with an Edge: Use Your Mind

http://www.amazon.com/Trade-Markets-Traders-World-Online-ebook/dp/B00KTQJV50

If you don't have the mind of a top trader, this book might be able to help you develop one. The writers in this book are very experienced and they are here to help you to be successful. Each of them has their own expertise in trading. What you need to do is to read the entire book and find the trader that fits your own trading style and grab it and make it your own. It is just that simple.

Find Success

This book presents to you the best trading strategies of these traders so that you might be able to select those that fit you best and then implement them into your own trading style.

In this book you'll learn:

1) How these expert traders make money and why

2) How to develop your own trading strategy

3) How to improve your trading psychology

4) How to be the trader you always wanted to be. You'll also learn how to avoid the losers and get rid of emotional attachment to trades. To be successful you need to learn to dump the losers quickly and keep the winners for big moves. Another thing this book does it that it gives you the desire to make continuous profits just like the master traders do.

Making profits one after another gives you a fantastic feeling which is tremendous!

Tips for Success

Also in this book you will know who to listen to for ideas from people who have many years of experience and who are seasoned traders.

Crucial Factors

In this book learn about crucial factors in the markets that many experts won't tell you about regarding time, volume and little known indicators. You'll know the right factors that can make you a profitable trader. The unique viewpoints from these many traders can explain why many traders lose and that can help you. The book was designed to help you develop your own trading edge in the markets to put you above others who don't have an edge and just trade by the seat of their pants.

Best Trading Strategies

http://www.amazon.com/Best-Trading-Strategies-Futures-Markets-ebook/dp/B00GG94F78

This is one of the most fascinating books that was ever written about trading because it is written by over thirty expert traders. These traders have many years of experience and they have learned how to turn technical analysis into profits in the markets. This is extremely difficult to do and if you have ever tried to trade the markets with technical analysis you would know what I mean. These writers have some of the best trading strategies they use and have the conviction and the discipline to act assertively and pull the buy or sell trigger regardless of pressures they have against them. They have presented these strategies at the Traders World Online Expo #14 in video presentations and in this book.

What sets these traders apart from other traders? Many think that beating the markets has something to do with discovering and using some secret formula. The traders in this book have the right attitude and many employ a combination of fundamental analysis, technical analysis principles and formulas in their best trading strategies.

Trading is one of the best ways to make a lot of money in the world if one does it right. One needs to find successful trading strategies and implement them in their own trading method. The purpose of this book is to present to you the best trading strategies of these traders so that you might be able to select those that fit you best and then implement them into your own trading.

I wish to express my appreciation to all the writers in this book who made the book possible. They have spent many hours of their time and hard work in writing their section of the book and the putting together their video presentation for the online expo.

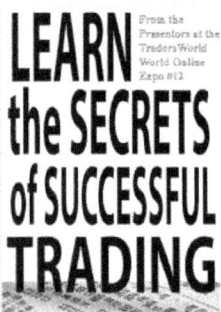

Learn the Secrets of Successful Trading

http://www.amazon.com/Secrets-Successful-Trading-Traders-Online-ebook/dp/B00A2ZIJQ0

Learn specific trading strategies to improve your trading, learn trading ideas and tactics to be more profitable, better optimize your trading system, find the fatal flaws in your trading, understand and use Elliott Wave to strengthen your trading, position using correct sizing to trade more profitable, understand Mercury cycles in trading the S&P, get consistently profitable trade setups, reduce risk and increase profits using volume, detect and trade the hidden market cycles, short term trading by taking the money and running, develop your mind for trading, overcoming Fear in Trading, trade with the smart money following volume, understand and use the Ultimate Oscillator, use high power trading with geometry, get better entries, understand the three legs to trading, use technical analysis with NinjaTrader 7, use a breakout system with cycles for greater returns with less risk, use Turn Signal for better entries and exits, trade with an edge, use options profitably, learn to trade online, map supply and demand on charts, quantify and execute portfolio rotation for auto trading.

Written by Many Expert Traders

The book was written by a large group of 35 expert traders, with high qualifications, most of who trade professionally and/or offer trading services and expensive courses to their clients. Some of them charge thousands of dollars per day for personal trading! These expert traders give generally 45-minute presentations covering the same topics given in this book at the Traders World Online Expo #12. By combining their talents in this book, they introduce a new dimension to finding a profitable trading edge in the market. You can use ideas and techniques of this group of experts to leverage your ability to find an edge to successfully trade. Using a group of experts in this manner to insure your trading success is unprecedented.

You'll never find a book like this anywhere! This unique trading book will help you uncover the underlying reasons for your lack of consistency in trading and will help you overcome poor habits that cost you money in trading. It will help you to expose the myths of the market one by one teaching you the right way to trade and to understand the realities of risk and to be comfortable with trading with market. The book is priceless!

Parallels to the Traders World Online Expo 12

The articles in this book exactly parallel the video presentations given at the Traders World Online Expo #12. This expo joins these top trading experts together with active traders looking for trading strategies & specific recommendations to help them profit in the markets and is held online at TradersWorldOnlineExpo.com.

From the DVD you'll learn: Time and Price Points; Consistently Profitable Trade Setups; How to Control Fear of Trading; Detecting and Trading Hidden Market Cycles; Position Sizing; Detailed Analysis of the S&P Market, 3 Keys to be a System Trader, Trading with an Edge, Lift off Trading Systems, Monetizing your Trading Expertise; Tracking Smart Money; Trading Price Cycles, Using Options, Mastering Trading with NinjaTrader; Learning Andrews Trading and much more.

Finding Your Trading Method

http://www.amazon.com/Finding-Trading-Method-Traders-Online-ebook/dp/B00DAIOL0E

Finding your trading method is the main problem you need to solve if you want to become a successful trader. You may be asking yourself, can I find my own trading method that will reflect my own personality toward trading? For example, do you have the patience to sit in front of a computer and trade all day? Do you prefer to swing trade from 3-5 days or do you like to hold positions for weeks and even months? Every trader is different. You need to find your own trading method.

Finding out your trading method is extremely important to produce a profitable benchmark that can be replicated in your live account. Perhaps the best way to find a successful trading method is to listen to many expert traders to understand what they have done to be successful. The best way to do that is to listen to the Traders World Online Expos presentations. This book duplicates what these experts have said in their presentations, which explains what they have done to find their own trading method.

If you have a trading method that gives you a predictable profit, then that type of objectivity contributes to your trading edge. The problem with most traders is that being inconsistent will never allow them to have an edge. After you find your trading method that you feel comfortable with, you must have the following:

An overall plan to:

1) Set your rule set and plan and then stick with it in all of your trading.

2) To give you a trading plan for every day.

The trade plan then should:

1) Have an exact entry price

2) Have a stop price

3) Have a way to add positions

4) Tell you where to take profits

5) Have a way to protect your profits

By reviewing all the methods given in this book by the expert traders, it will give, you the preliminary steps that you need to find your footing in finding your own trading method.

Reading this book and by seeing the actual recorded presentations on the Traders World Online Expo site can act as a reference tool for selecting your method of trading, investment strategies and tactics.

It took many of these expert traders in this book 15 – 30 years to finally come up and find the answers to find their trading method to make consistent profit. Finding your trading method could be then much easier when you read this book and incorporate the techniques that best fit your personality and style from these traders. This book will enable you to that fastest way to do that.

So if you want help to find your own trading method to be successful in the markets then buy and read this book.

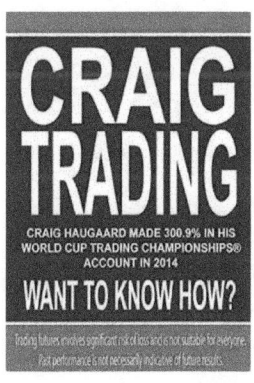

CRAIG TRADING: Craig Haugaard made 300.9% in his World Cup Trading Championships® Account in 2014 - Want to Know How?

http://www.amazon.com/CRAIG-TRADING-Haugaard-Trading-Championships%C2%AE-ebook/dp/B00WT2CO7Y

This book contains an interview that I made with Craig Haugaard, third-place finisher in the 2014 World Cup Championship of

Futures Trading® with a 300.9% net profit. I asked him many questions on exactly how he did it.

In the rest of the book I explain to you how to use the indicators that Craig used to make his 300.9% return.

Here are the indicators that he used:

• Seasonality

• MACD

• Stochastics

• Moving Averages

• Trailing Stops

• Fibonacci Retracements & Extensions

All of the charts in this book are produced using my favorite charting software Market-Analyst®. I have also arranged for you to get a FREE trial so that you might have the chance to actually work with these indicators with a real charting platform.

You will also be able to view the video presentations that I personally created so you can see how these indicators can be setup and followed with clear and concise step-by-step instructions.

Market-Analyst
Moving Averages
Cycles
Seasonality
Volume
Patterns
Williams %R
Chandelier Stops

After you understand how these indicators work, I would then recommend that you go to WorldCupAdvisor.com and consider following Michael Cook's real-time trades.

This one-of-a-kind book teaches you how to identify the direction of the markets and trade the markets by using popular trading indicators. This is done by concise instructions backed by learning videos, hands on practice with real trading software and by following real-time trades of a master trader.

www.ingramcontent.com/pod-product-compliance
Lightning Source LLC
Chambersburg PA
CBHW051911170526
45168CB00001B/336